THE CONSUMER'S GUIDE TO
NEW JERSEY PERSONAL INJURY CLAIMS

GARRY R. SALOMON
Attorney at Law

ISBN: 1453720499
ISBN-13: 9781453720493
Library of Congress Control Number: 2010911025

Garry R. Salomon *
Attorney at Law
Davis, Saperstein & Salomon, P.C.
375 Cedar Lane
Teaneck, NJ 07666
US National Telephone Number : 1-800-529-2000
garry.salomon@dsslaw.com

* Certified by the Supreme Court of New Jersey as a Civil Trial Attorney

DEDICATION

This book is dedicated to my wife, Jayne, and my three sons, Michael, Jason, and Jeffrey who patiently waited for me to arrive home on too many nights and weekends while I learned the valuable lessons contained in this book.

I also dedicate this book to my law partners

Samuel L. Davis, Marc C. Saperstein, Steven Benvenisti, and Paul A. Garfield, who continually inspire me with their knowledge and passion each day as they diligently advocate on behalf of their clients.

Special thanks also go to my staff and associates, many of whom choose to work with the injured for their personal satisfaction.

I especially appreciate the conscientious assistance of Jeffrey E. Salomon, Alexa Davis, and Daniel Silbert who assisted me in the final editing of this book.

Finally, to my past and current clients:

It has been a true honor and privilege to be of service to you and your families.

ABOUT THE AUTHOR

Garry R. Salomon has practiced law in New Jersey since 1977. During the past three decades, he has helped thousands of people and families affected by almost every type of personal injury claim imaginable.

After graduating Bergenfield High School, he attended Fairleigh Dickinson University, where in 1974 he received his Bachelor of Science Degree in Accounting. After working briefly for a big eight accounting firm, he entered law school. Three years later, he received his Juris Doctor degree from the University of Akron. In 1977, he was admitted to the New Jersey bar and began his law practice.

Garry Salomon is a founding member and serves as the managing director of Davis, Saperstein & Salomon, P.C. His main practice areas of concentration include all areas of personal injury law. He particularly enjoys the courtroom environment and concentrates on bringing his cases to the trial stage. His courtroom experience qualified him to become certified by the Supreme Court of New Jersey as a Certified Civil Trial Attorney, a designation held by less than 3 percent of all of New Jersey's licensed lawyers.

Although most of his cases are resolved prior to trial, he has been quoted as saying,

An insurance company will consider paying fair and just compensation only if they see that the plaintiff is ready to let a jury decide the case. However, if an insurance company is unwilling to deal fairly with the plaintiff, I then trust a jury to decide the outcome.

Garry Salomon has consistently given back to the legal community by being an active member of the American Association for Justice and The New Jersey Association for Justice (NJAJ). He currently is an officer of NJAJ, New Jersey's largest trial lawyers association, and has been appointed to its Board of Governors for the past twelve consecutive years.

On February 25, 2006, Garry Salomon presented a lecture to the attendees of the NJAJ Pines Seminar entitled "Summation: Bringing it Home." In conjunction with the seminar, the *New Jersey Lawyer* published an article with the same title authored by Mr. Salomon.

Garry Salomon has served as Co-Chairman and program chair for NJAJ's Trial Academy, where he has lectured on "The Art of Direct Examination." He also has lectured at NJAJ's annual Boardwalk Convention. He founded and acts as co-moderator and co-chairperson of the 2000–2010 annual "Litigation at Sunrise" Boardwalk Seminar. In 2008, Garry R. Salomon was honored to be selected as a member of NJAJ's "Dream Team," which demonstrated the proper methods to employ when trying automobile accident cases. On November 13, 2009, together with his partner Marc Saperstein, he moderated a seminar entitled "Trial Evidence" at NJAJ's annual Meadowlands Seminar.

PROFESSIONAL ASSOCIATIONS

American Association of Justice (formerly ATLA)
      Motor Vehicle Accident Section
      Medical Malpractice Section
      Civil Rights Section
      Employment Rights Section
      Trucking Accident Section

New Jersey Association for Justice (NJAJ)
    Formerly Association of Trial Lawyers of America-N.J.
      Treasurer 2010–2011
      Secretary 2009–2010
      Officer-Assistant Secretary 2008–2009
      Statewide Membership Chair 1997–2009
      Trial Academy Co-Chair 1998–1999
      Board of Governors 1997–2010
      Executive Committee 2009–2010
      Automobile Reparations Committee
      Long Range Planning & Finance Committees 2010

SuperLawyers (As selected by *Law & Politics Magazine*)
      2006, 2007, 2008, 2009, 2010* [1]

Million Dollar Advocates Forum

---

[1]   The reference to SuperLawyers by an attorney in a publication requires the following disclaimer language: "No aspect of this advertisement has been approved by the Supreme Court of New Jersey."

The American Trial Lawyers Association (Top 100 Lawyers)

Other Associations and Affiliations

Bergen County Bar Association
New Jersey State Bar Association
American Bar Association
Teaneck Bar Association Founder 2003-2010
TANJ Trial Attorneys of New Jersey
American Academy of Trial Advocacy
Teaneck Chamber of Commerce Trustee
"Businessman of the Year 2007 Award"
Public Justice – Member
Truth in Justice – Contributor and Member 2009
NJAJ Legal PAC
The Melvin Belli Society
National Crime Victims Association

BAR ADMISSIONS:

State of New Jersey 1977
United States District Court 1977
United States Supreme Court 1982
Certified as a Civil Trial Attorney
by the NJ Supreme Court

AREAS OF EXPERTISE:

Civil Jury Trials
Personal Injury and Wrongful Death Cases
Catastrophic Injury Cases
Injuries to Children
Motor Vehicle Accidents
Automobile Accidents

Motorcycle and Bicycle Accidents
Pedestrian Accidents
Truck and Eighteen-Wheeler Accidents
Premises Liability and Slip, Trip and Fall Cases
Ice and Snow-Related Accidents
Supermarket and Store Accidents
Mass Tort and Pharmaceutical Cases
Spinal Injury and Catastrophic Injury Cases
Medical, Nursing, and Legal Malpractice Cases
Criminal Law and Criminal Defense
Legal Malpractice Cases
Animal Attacks and Dog Bite Cases
Machine and Defective Product Cases
Inadequate Security Cases
Workers' Compensation

On the personal side, Garry is married and is the father of three sons. He enjoys skiing, boating, and cycling and he has earned a black belt in Shotokan Karate. He particularly enjoys playing the blues on his "Gold Top" Gibson Les Paul guitar.

ABOUT DAVIS, SAPERSTEIN & SALOMON, P.C.

For over thirty years, the partners of Davis, Saperstein and Salomon, P.C., a professional corporation, have been representing the injured in courtrooms throughout America. The firm was originally founded in 1981 by Samuel L. Davis and Marc C. Saperstein. Six years later, Garry R. Salomon joined his two childhood friends as a partner in the firm.

Throughout most of its existence, the firm has exclusively represented plaintiffs in personal injury cases. The firm does not represent any insurance companies, but has extensive litigation experience against almost all of the largest insurance companies in America.

The firm reached national recognition when, during the '90s, partner Marc C. Saperstein, a former President of the Association of Trial Lawyers of America – New Jersey Chapter, participated as a member of the trial team against Big Tobacco. He later joined the trial team fighting and litigating against American Home Products on behalf of thousands of patients injured by its harmful diet drug Fen-Phen.

Partner Samuel L. Davis has also achieved national recognition for his work in connection with defective orthopedic medical devices. Always an innovator in the legal field, Sam Davis was the first lawyer to use the Internet to allow a bedridden paralyzed quadriplegic client to participate in his trial.

Through the years, the firm has had the privilege of representing over twenty thousand injured clients and has recovered hundreds of millions of dollars in verdicts or settlements on their behalf.

More recently, Certified Civil Trial Attorneys Paul A. Garfield and Steven Benvenisti were named as partners of the firm. Steven Benvenisti is a nationally recognized motivational speaker, having miraculously made a full recovery from catastrophic injuries suffered in 1989 as a result of being struck by a drunk driver as a pedestrian.

The firm continued to grow and represents the injured in all twenty-one of New Jersey's counties as well as the New York metropolitan area. Currently the firm employs over forty professional and nonprofessional staff members, all hired to serve the needs of its personal injury clients.

Aside from its legal accomplishments, the firm has also been recognized for its civic and charitable work. Several times a year, the lawyers of Davis, Saperstein & Salomon, P.C., will speak or moderate a legal educational seminar as part of the legal profession's mandatory continuing legal education requirements.

The firm prides itself on never charging a consultation fee and charging a legal fee only if a case is won.

In addition to fighting for justice in the courtroom, the firm also advocates for continued and fairer consumer rights by reminding the lawmakers of the plight of the injured, the disabled, and the less fortunate.

TABLE OF CONTENTS

IMPORTANT NOTICES

This book is designed to give you general information regarding personal injury claims and lawsuits in New Jersey. It is not intended to give you personalized legal advice. The area of law commonly called "tort law" is extremely complex. In fact, few lawyers have sufficient medical or courtroom training and experience to even venture into handling these cases.

Nothing in this book should be construed as specific legal advice, since all cases are fact sensitive and unique. In order for lawyers to give legal advice, you must consult with them directly. If you decide to pursue your claim and a lawyer expressly decides to accept your case, you may "retain" him or her as your legal counsel. You do this by entering into an agreement, which in New Jersey must be in writing.

Accordingly, do not rely solely upon the contents of this book in making your decisions. Due to changes in the law, either through court decisions or by legislation, it is important that you consult with a competent and experienced personal injury lawyer before making any decisions.

This book is not intended to serve as a "do it yourself" manual to resolving your own personal injury claim. Experienced lawyers will certainly protect your interests and add significant value to any claim. In fact, few personal injury lawyers would even consider representing themselves if injured in an accident.

This book is not intended to interfere with any legal relationship you may now have. If counsel already represents you, this book may raise and answer certain questions that you may have. Please discuss these questions with your current lawyer. Each personal injury law firm practices law differently. If you are having a problem with your lawyer, meet with him or her and try to discuss the issues and work things out. If you lose confidence in your lawyer, you certainly can change counsel; however, this should be done only as a last resort.

FROM THE AUTHOR

I wrote this book for people who were injured because of someone else's negligence. Too often, these events are called "accidents" when, in fact, negligence was the real cause.

If you or someone you know has had the misfortune of being injured in New Jersey because of someone's negligence, then this book is the right book to read.

Although many people make jokes about lawsuits, rest assured that it's no laughing matter to those injured. As a result of being put in a position they did not bargain for, accident victims may feel anger and frustration. All too often, they just don't know what to do or where to go to preserve their rights. As an unfortunate consequence, they take no action and allow deadlines to pass, causing them to lose their valuable rights.

It is for those people, as well as my clients, that I wrote this book as both a reference source and a starting point in understanding what's ahead.

I also strongly believe that, without a doubt, honesty is the best policy for all people to follow. Be honest with your doctors and the lawyers involved in your case. Don't be afraid to tell your lawyer about any situations or problems you've had in the past. Dishonesty and lying are not acceptable options and they will only serve to discredit both you and your case.

INTRODUCTION

In 2008, there were 302,153 automobile accidents within the state of New Jersey in which 68,512 people suffered injuries.[2] Tragically, according to the U.S. Department of Transportation, 590 people died on New Jersey roads in 2008 because of car crashes. Statistically, a person has a one out of four chance of being involved in a car crash during his or her lifetime.

Each day, we read and hear about car accidents affecting our friends, families, and our celebrities. No one is immune to being involved in a car crash, not even royalty. Both Princess Diana and Princess Grace (Kelly) lost their lives because of car crashes. Numerous other famous stars and sports figures have been seriously injured or disfigured because of automobile accidents.

Some accident survivors are more fortunate than others; some can walk away from an accident without a scratch. Others, however, suffer life-changing injuries or even death despite there being little or no property damage to their cars.

The good news is that the number of people injured because of car accidents has steadily declined throughout the years. Newer cars are being designed to be safer, fewer people drink and drive and most people are safely buckled into their car seats.

Years ago, manufacturers did not install airbags or seatbelts. Dashboards were not padded, there were no headrests, and special safety glass was not installed. There were no child safety seats and cars were not designed with today's crash-resistant features such as energy-absorbing bumpers. Through the years, roadways have been

---

2   New Jersey Department of Transportation http://www.state.nj.us/transportation/refdata/accident

designed for safety first and are being maintained better. Restrictions have been placed on young drivers' privileges and the penalties for driving under the influence of alcohol have steadily increased.

Aside from automobile accidents, people suffer injuries, sometimes fatal, in other types of accidents. People still slip, trip, and fall in stores and on ice or snow. People still get injured on the job, are bitten by dogs, harmed by negligent doctors or hospitals, or suffer horrific side effects from dangerous medications. People and workers continue to suffer injuries due to defective and unsafe products, many of which are manufactured in foreign countries.

Although the federal and state governments may regulate, control, or punish offenders, they provide no direct remedy for those harmed to be fully compensated for all of their pain, suffering and financial losses (or, as lawyers would say, "be made whole" for their losses). They do, however, if all else fails, provide a legal system known as the civil justice system for unsettled disputes to be decided by juries. Although juries are without power to return an injured person to his or her previous state of health, they do have the power to award a sum of money to the injured in order to fairly compensate the person for their harms, losses, pain, and suffering. For most people, this will result in their first and only exposure to the legal system.

This book is about the New Jersey legal system as well as some of the basic first-year law school course known as *tort* law. The law of torts developed in England hundreds of years ago to prevent people from settling disputes among themselves in a violent fashion. Notably, even the Bible prescribed ways of compensating those harmed by the wrongful acts of others. In recent times, people have been aware of their social responsibility to make up for the harms and losses they cause to others by purchasing insurance, which compensates those injured and protects their own assets in case they are sued by those they harmed.

When someone is harmed, he or she has the right and expectation to be made whole for any losses. No one should apologize for using the courthouse to resolve an injury claim. It is a function of government guaranteed by the U.S. Constitution and available to all, whether they are U.S. citizens or not.

This book is designed to be a basic reference guide drawn from my thirty-plus years of experience representing accident victims. This book is by no means exhaustive of any one particular topic or area of tort law. Instead, it should serve to give some primary care guidance until the reader meets with a skilled personal injury lawyer. All injured readers should seek out a legal consultation, and if necessary, legal representation as soon as possible. From that point forward, clients will understand what they can expect and what is expected from them.

There is another strong reason why it is recommended that an accident victim seek immediate legal advice; laws are different in each state and are changing on a daily basis. Some of those changes in the law could affect a claimant's right to be compensated for their harms, losses, and other damages.

Despite efforts to prevent them, car accidents and their resulting injuries continue to happen. If you are reading this book, it is likely that either you or someone close to you was injured in a motor vehicle accident. This book is designed to help the accident victim navigate his or her way through this process and its minefields. Insurance adjusters and juries have turned away many people with perfectly good cases due to avoidable mistakes.

This book is not intended to be a replacement for hiring an attorney, nor is it intended to give legal advice. Proper legal advice can be given only after an attorney is familiar with all of the facts and circumstances of an individual's case. In other words, this book is intended only to help you stop the leak until the plumber arrives.

Although this book will help an accident victim avoid fatal mistakes, it does not address case strategy issues. Lawyers discuss these confidential issues with their clients behind closed doors. Issues such as jury selection, expert witness selection, case value, and settlement strategies are all important decisions to consider and make wisely.

From reading this book, you will be able to engage in an informed and intelligent conversation with your lawyer and ask the right questions in order to make correct and informed decisions. With the help of this book, you will learn some of the lessons I've learned over the past thirty years that have proven to be successful for so many of my clients.

In order to communicate information effectively, I will assume that you or a close family member was involved in an accident, which is why I address the book's comments to you individually. This information will be helpful to you in learning how to proceed, whether you have had an accident or not.

CHAPTER ONE

LIFE IS BEAUTIFUL

It's a beautiful day. You get up to start what you expect will be a normal day. Your health is good; you have no major aches or pains. In fact, you got an excellent report from your doctor at your last physical just two years ago. You have a good job that you enjoy, and most of all, you value your free time to engage in the things you've learned to love.

On that same day, you get into your car, fasten your seat belt, and you proceed to drive down the same road on the same route you've traveled every working day for the past five years. As you approach the familiar intersection of Main and Elm, you slow down and come to a complete stop behind another car already stopped for a red light. Suddenly, an SUV violently rear-ends you, pushing your car forward into the rear of the car directly in front of you.

The force of the impact causes you to be jolted backward, violently striking the back of your skull against the headrest. You then lunge forward while your pelvis is firmly and "safely" secured tightly against the seat bottom, after which you are again jolted backward into your seat. Your car then comes to a stop.

You look forward and all you see is the front of your car firmly implanted into the rear of the car directly in front of you. Your mind is racing and you think about how this has now messed up your day. Little did you know or could you anticipate how this accident would affect your overall health and happiness. Suddenly, you are thrust into the world of both the medical and legal systems.

Ambulance attendants remove you from your car and put you onto a stretcher. While your car is towed away, an ambulance takes you to the local hospital. Four hours later, you are discharged with a hospital bill, a prescription, and follow-up instructions. You now go home feeling awful and in pain. You are now a patient and a client. Good luck, because you will need it.

CHAPTER TWO

THE PROCESS BEGINS

You arrive home feeling extremely tired, in pain, and you decide that you are going to just sleep it off. As you toss and turn in bed, you find no comfort in any position. In desperation, you take the pills prescribed by the hospital's attending physician. A few hours later, you wake up from a nap with more pain and a stiff neck. You stand up and suddenly, you feel pain in your lower back. Still feeling exhausted, you now feel discomfort from the glare of bright kitchen lights as you ponder what to do about the intense headache you've developed. You now think about your work schedule for tomorrow and then it occurs to you that you have no way to get to work since your beloved car has been wrecked. "What the heck," you figure, "I'll just take off an extra sick day." After a night of tossing and turning, you wake up with much more pain, a worse headache, and you are now finding that you are unable to move your head at all.

You then call your doctor and she tells you that she can see you in two weeks. All you want is to be checked out. The phone rings and it's your insurance company asking you about how the accident happened. You wonder, "How do they already know about this accident?" The caller then informs you that the driver of the car in front of you already reported the accident to his insurance carrier and that you rear-ended their insured. You immediately protest and tell this apathetic person that you are outraged at the accusation that you caused the accident. The insurance representative then transfers you to another department of Allfarm Insurance and you are put on hold for ten minutes listening to the same message: "Please continue to hold for a representative. All of our customer care agents are busy. Please continue…" Finally, you are able to give a statement regarding your claim when you are transferred to another department to open up a file for personal injury protection benefits. Thirty-two minutes later you have become claim number 2XZYF437J-010.

Intending to rest up in order to be fully ready for Saturday morning golf, you stay in bed when the phone rings. "Hello, this is Bayville Salvage Company. We towed your wreck to our lot and we just want to let you know that our daily storage fee is $55 per day, including partial days."

You then ask about your briefcase and they tell you that they are not responsible for personal contents left in any car. Didn't you read the sign on the tow truck? "Not responsible for personal contents."

Your boss now calls and asks about next week's business trip to Chicago. Being under the influence of several narcotic painkillers, you abruptly say to him, "I'll let you know later on this week." You hang up and realize that today is Friday. Two hours later, your boss calls and tells you to take as much time off as you need and not to worry because Jones will cover Chicago for you. "Why Jones?" you think. "I hate that little smartass punk." You continue to spend the rest of the day in bed, in and out of consciousness. The next day you wake up in even more pain with numbness down your legs.

At 10:00 a.m. a letter carrier arrives and drops off four letters from law offices soliciting you to "act now" and sign with them. Sue? "I'm not that kind of person," you think to yourself. You have now consumed all of your pain medication from the hospital and you still have not seen a doctor.

You discuss this with your spouse, who tells you to call your lawyer. You have known your lawyer since he did a real estate closing for you when you first got married. He makes an appointment to see you later next week. He has just too many closings and divorce consultations to fit you in this week. You figure there's no urgency and so you make an appointment to see him at the end of next week.

Satisfied that you have taken some action by making an appointment with a lawyer, you rest assured that things will work out OK for you in the future. "Why wouldn't it work out?" you think to yourself. "The accident wasn't my fault, I didn't do anything wrong."

The truth is that your case should succeed if you make the correct decisions, undergo appropriate medical care, and most importantly, hire the most appropriate lawyer for the job.

The process has now begun. Most people believe that just as they had no control over the occurrence of the accident, they have no control over the outcome of the personal injury claim. However, the truth is that clients have an enormous amount of control over the outcome. That control clearly does not require exaggerating or "spinning" a case. The control a client has is in being educated about the ways to avoid unknowingly sabotaging their own case by making avoidable mistakes. Fortunately, this book will help you avoid those mistakes while making an honest, clear, and valuable claim for your injuries.

Over the next few days following an accident, an accident victim has many issues to face and many important decisions to make. These decisions include medical decisions, legal decisions, property damage claims, transportation decisions, work-related decisions, and decisions affecting social plans and events.

An accident victim should not make these decisions in a vacuum. Instead, he or she should make decisions by knowing and understanding the rules, concepts, and realties of the claims process. These rules, concepts, and realities will be discussed in this book and highlighted in bold print at the end of each chapter. Be certain to pay close attention to them and be certain to understand them. Most importantly, be aware of these principles when you make your decisions.

In any personal injury claim, it is the injured person's obligation to prove his or her case. Cases are not won on the facts alone. Cases are won based on those facts that are relevant, proven, and admissible in a court of law. For example, in some states, and in certain situations in New Jersey, if a person suffers back pain because of a car accident, he or she may be required to prove in court that the back pain resulted from an identifiable injury that appears on an MRI film, and that the accident more likely than not caused it.

CHAPTER THREE

INSURANCE COMPANIES

Insurance companies are in business to collect insurance premiums and make profit. They are not in business to pay claims. Insurance companies are private businesses whose purpose is to protect their insurance policyholders' assets by assuming the risk of paying for unexpected losses. Types of consumer's insurance policies include automobile coverage to pay for unintentional injuries to others, property damage and medical expenses; life insurance, disability insurance, homeowner's insurance, and medical insurance.

To insurance companies, the payment of any claim is called a "loss." Each dollar paid by an insurance company will reduce their profit by a dollar. The opposite is also true; every loss dollar not paid out is an additional dollar of profit. Insurance companies make their profit by denying claims, reducing payments, or not paying claims at all.

Insurance companies represent the interests of their policyholders and not those harmed or those bringing claims against their policyholders. This bit of information is extremely important to know when approached by a representative of an insurance company. Do not be fooled. Although they may appear to be concerned, caring, and apologetic, they are merely gathering information to set a reserve for your claim. Be very careful; they are recording you and they are looking for facts that can be used against you in the future to minimize their future payout. At their urging, many people consent to giving recorded statements. These recorded conversations can certainly come back to haunt you.

Under the terms of your insurance policy, you are obligated to cooperate with your own automobile insurance company by giving them a statement, as well as information pertaining to your injuries. Depending upon the terms of your insurance policy, your carrier will set up a claim file for medical benefits, collision, or for additional insurance coverage. If you do not provide them with such information, they can deny your claim for failing to do so.

Don't be surprised if you receive a call or visit by an insurance company representative who may be either an investigator or an insurance company adjuster. Be careful of what you say. If you have already hired a lawyer, under no circumstances should you speak to any of them without the consent of your lawyer.

Likewise, a key defense used by insurance companies at the time of trial is to show that a desire to win a lawsuit guided your decisions and actions. It is extremely important not to give others the impression that you are motivated by money. Don't even make any jokes to an insurance adjuster since the literal meaning of your joke, written in a claim file, can be quite different than what you intended.

If the person who caused the accident said anything to you about how the accident happened, including an apology, write down the exact words with the date and time he or she made those admissions.

Conversations between you and your spouse as well as conversations between you and your attorneys are privileged and confidential, which means that you need not disclose them to anyone. However, all conversations with anyone else can be what lawyers call "discovered" and used against you later.

SUMMARY

RULE: INSURANCE COMPANIES ARE IN BUSINESS TO COLLECT INSURANCE PREMIUMS AND TO MAKE A PROFIT. THEY ARE NOT IN BUSINESS TO PAY CLAIMS.

RULE: YOU SHOULD NOT TALK TOO MUCH ABOUT YOUR CASE TO ANYONE EXCEPT AN EXPERIENCED AND QUALIFIED PERSONAL INJURY LAWYER.

CHAPTER FOUR

THE ACCIDENT

Depending on one's physical condition, what occurs at the accident scene is of critical importance. Assumptions will be made by others. Questions will be answered without thought. Tempers may flare and mistakes will be made.

Generally, if a person believes he or she is injured, that person should remain in the car, provided that the car is not located in a dangerous position. The best advice we can give is the following:

RULE: UNDER NO CIRCUMSTANCES SHOULD YOU EVER GET OUT OF YOUR CAR AND STAND BEHIND IT TO DISCUSS THE ACCIDENT OR PROPERTY DAMAGE.

<u>We Repeat:</u>

RULE: UNDER NO CIRCUMSTANCES SHOULD YOU EVER GET OUT OF YOUR CAR AND STAND BEHIND IT TO DISCUSS THE ACCIDENT OR PROPERTY DAMAGE.

Why do we repeat this bolded statement? We do that because you have two legs. Unfortunately, perhaps the most tragic type of unnecessary injury at an accident scene occurs when a third car crashes into the second car pushing it again into the first car. People standing between those cars can lose their limbs or even their lives. A better practice is to turn on the emergency flashers, leave the vehicle, and stand as far away from the accident scene as possible until the police arrive and secure the area.

Do not allow the other driver to convince you to handle the situation without the police or insurance company's involvement.

Quite often at accident scenes, the negligent driver is extremely upset. He or she is not upset about the changes and inconveniences that are about to occur in your life. What that driver is upset about is that he or she may receive a summons and a likely increase in his or her auto insurance rates.

Furthermore, the at-fault driver may give you a false identity, may have stolen the car, and may lie about the facts or even dispute that this particular accident caused the property damage. Don't be concerned about that. Instead, be concerned about protecting your own interests.

Furthermore, in many states, it is mandatory to file a police report if property damage is over a certain amount. In New Jersey, that amount is $500.[3] So, be certain to call the police to the accident scene and wait patiently for them to arrive.

Do not engage in small talk with the other driver or offer him or her any anecdotes to make them feel better about the accident. Instead, look around for potential eyewitnesses and get their names, addresses, and phone numbers. If you have a cell phone with a camera, be certain to photograph their license plates just in case you receive wrong information. Don't count on the police to investigate an accident scene for eyewitnesses. They are more interested in securing the area for safety, doing a report, and resuming the normal traffic flow as quickly as possible. Do not be surprised if the police report contains inaccuracies.

---

3   If you are a driver involved in an accident resulting in injury to or death of any one person or damage to property in excess of five hundred dollars ($500), you must report this accident to the Security Responsibility Accident Reporting Section, Division of Motor Vehicles, NJSA 39:4-130.

Do not be afraid to take pictures of the accident scene, the other driver, the license plates, eyewitnesses, and property damage to all cars involved in the accident.

Professional drivers such as truckers are trained in what to say and do at an accident scene. For years, they carried disposable cameras to document potential losses themselves. In fact, some lawyers are on twenty-four-hour call and pre-retained by truckers to travel immediately to an accident scene in the event of a crash. That way, a negligent trucker will not speak to a police officer unless his or her attorney is present. All investigation and statements made to that lawyer would be confidential and subject to attorney-client privilege.

Just as a trucker is not embarrassed to take photos, you should not be either. If someone else is available at the accident scene, give that person your camera or cell phone to take the photos. Your car may have minimum damage and that minimum damage can be used against you. But remember, it may improve your case to show significant property damage to the offending driver's vehicle. Often insurance companies will conveniently lose those photos or not even take those pictures if they believe such photos would be damaging to their case.

Likewise, over the next few days, photographs of scars, injuries, and black-and-blue marks can be extremely important and persuasive in proving an injury.

If no police officer arrives at the scene, make sure you take down the name, address, and phone number of the driver. Do not let him or her write it down; instead copy it down yourself directly from his or her license, registration, and insurance card. Take photographs of those documents with your camera phone or camera. You must also give the other driver the same information about yourself.

Even if you are feeling fine at the accident scene, do not offer that you are not hurt. Many times the effects from the injuries may take hours or days to present themselves. Statements that you were not hurt will undoubtedly be extremely harmful, as they will be used to disprove your claim.

If the police officer suggests calling an ambulance, you need to take the officer's advice. The officer may detect a physical or emotional condition in you that appears to be abnormal. It's always best to take an officer's advice at the accident scene regarding medical treatment.

SUMMARY

RULE: UNDER NO CIRCUMSTANCES SHOULD YOU EVER GET OUT OF YOUR CAR AND STAND BEHIND IT TO DISCUSS THE ACCIDENT OR PROPERTY DAMAGE.

RULE: DO NOT ALLOW THE OTHER DRIVER TO CONVINCE YOU TO HANDLE THE SITUATION WITHOUT THE POLICE OR INSURANCE COMPANIES.

RULE: DO NOT BE AFRAID TO TAKE PICTURES OF THE ACCIDENT SCENE, THE OTHER DRIVER, AND PROPERTY DAMAGE TO THE CARS.

RULE: DO NOT OFFER ANY INFORMATION TO THE OTHER DRIVER CONCERNING THE EXTENT OF YOUR INJURIES.

CHAPTER FIVE

POLICE REPORTS

This may come as a shock, but it's very common for police reports to contain false assumptions and wrong conclusions.

One would think that the official police report would certainly be an accurate investigation as to the cause of an accident. That assumption is false. All too often, police officers dispatched to the accident scene, make observations, and quickly jot down a few notes. Officers are primarily concerned about clearing the area to allow the normal flow of traffic. They do not particularly enjoy the paperwork that results from accidents. No young police officer ever went into law enforcement dreaming about one day being able to write accident reports. As a result, they tend to try to gather the information and complete their reports as quickly as possible, often at the expense of thoroughly investigating the accident scene.

Police officers instantly judge the credibility of the parties and formulate a conclusion. They may then issue a report or issue a summons to the driver that they believe is at fault. The only problem is that the police officers did not see the actual accident and conducted only a quick superficial investigation. Be sure to write down the officers' names and badge numbers. You will also need to know which law enforcement agency employs them.

You will not get a police report at the accident scene; instead, officers will advise you when to pick up the report. In New Jersey, if the accident occurred on an interstate roadway, the reporting agency will be the New Jersey State Police. If it's on a county roadway, the reporting agency could be the county police or the local township's police department.

If there is an error in the police report or if you disagree with the police officer's explanation of how the accident happened, especially if an unknown vehicle caused the accident, you should immediately file an amendment to the police report. Your lawyers can assist you in properly drafting your explanation as to how the accident happened. Be aware, however, that often after a police report is finalized, the police are reluctant to change the report. You may need to speak with the captain in order to be permitted to file a statement to be added to the report.

When you get the police report, you will see boxes around the edges filled in with numbers that are part of a code. These numbers come from a police report grid. The numbers will reflect certain key facts regarding the nature of the accident, the cause, information about the participants and even which parts of the cars were damaged. You need to ask for and receive a copy of this grid. The local municipality grid may differ from that of the State Police report grid. For your convenience, a copy of the current local grid appears in Appendix A of this book.

If the police issued a motor vehicle summons or a ticket to the "at-fault driver," you may be called to testify as a witness in that municipal court hearing. If you are called to testify in court, you will do so in connection with the prosecution of the other driver. Again, you are merely a witness to this prosecution. The "burden of proof" in a traffic violation case is the same as in any criminal case, which means that the judge must find the at-fault driver guilty "beyond a reasonable doubt." The municipal court is not concerned with your injuries, your pain, or your damages. The court's sole function is to decide whether state laws were broken. If the defendant is convicted, the court must then impose a punishment that may result in points and a fine.

Since the burden of proof in a personal injury case is a "preponderance of evidence," the findings of the municipal court are usually not relevant or admissible as proof of fault in your personal injury case. As a result, often, a lawyer will advise you not to pursue the municipal court case since your testimony at the time of trial can be used to point out inconsistencies in your future claims. If you are called to court, consult with an attorney immediately.

It is also important that you know that a motor vehicle summons can be issued only within the first thirty days after a motor vehicle accident. If for some reason you receive a ticket signed by the officer or the other driver(s), you should consider going to the police station and issuing a summons against the other driver. Do this only after talking with your attorney.

SUMMARY

RULE: IT IS VERY COMMON FOR POLICE REPORTS TO CONTAIN FALSE ASSUMPTIONS AND WRONG CONCLUSIONS.

RULE: ERRORS IN THE POLICE REPORT NEED TO BE CORRECTED AS SOON AS POSSIBLE.

RULE: CONVICTIONS OF MOTOR VEHICLE OFFENSES IN MUNICIPAL COURT ARE NOT LIKELY GOING TO BE ADMITTED INTO EVIDENCE IN A LATER PERSONAL INJURY TRIAL FOR DAMAGES.

CHAPTER SIX

PROPERTY DAMAGE

If your car was damaged or totaled, do not dispose of or repair your car without having the at-fault driver's insurance company evaluate the damage and provide an estimate of repair. Do not transfer title of the vehicle to them or give them the car without taking detailed photographs of both external property damage and non-visible frame or internal bumper damage. Digital images are preferable since you can e-mail them to your lawyer's office easily or send them in a digital format.

If your car is impounded or is being held in a storage facility where you have no access to it, you need to call them as soon as possible to gain access in order to have the car photographed. Most reputable law firms have investigators on call to secure photographs of the property damage of both your vehicle and that of the defendant.

Copies of all property damage estimates as well as all car rental receipts should be saved as proof of financial damages. You may also give copies of these expenses to the appropriate property damage adjuster.

If your car was covered by collision coverage, you can elect to have your own insurance company adjust the loss and pay for your repairs. They will then contact the other driver's insurance company for reimbursement and try to get your deductible paid back to you as well. You may need to be patient since the claims process to collect back your deductible may take several months.

If you owned the car that was damaged or totaled because of the accident, your lawyers may allow you to negotiate your property loss claim directly with the negligent driver's insurance carrier. Insurance companies are responsible to pay only the value for your loss based on any one of three valuation methods approved by the New Jersey Commission of Banking and Insurance.

The three valuation methods are as follows:

1. Taking the average of the retail values of substantially similar vehicles listed by an approved used automobile valuation service, such as the current edition of "Auto Blue Book" and "NADA home page used car guide."

2. Using a quote obtained by the insurance company for a substantially similar vehicle available for you to purchase from a dealer located within twenty-five miles of where your car is normally garaged; or.

3. Using the services of an approved source, that may include a computerized database service such as ADP or CCC in order to determine the market value.

If your car cannot be accurately valued by any one of the above three methods because they fail to accurately represent a true cross section of the marketplace, then the insurance company is required to use the best available method and provide a written explanation as to how they calculated their valuation. They must also provide you with an itemized list showing all additions and reductions for prior damage. They are also obligated to add the sales tax to their offer.

If your car is leased, the insurance company will be responsible for paying the value of your car to the leasing company. But be aware that under certain lease circumstances, you may not have sufficient coverage to pay the full balance of the lease due to finance charge rules. Hopefully, you will be covered under what's known as GAP insurance, which pays the difference in the book value of the car and the balance of the lease payments owed. This is not automatic coverage, but read your lease since you may have purchased GAP coverage as part of your lease agreement.

If property damage losses are not resolved in a timely fashion, you may then become responsible for storage charges. It's important to select your repair facility in order to avoid personal responsibility for storage charges at the tow facility. Generally, insurance companies will pay for a reasonable amount of tow yard storage charges. However, an insurance company can stop paying for storage if they give you an opportunity to move your car to a body shop or junkyard, but they must give you at least three days of advance notice.

If you receive a check for the damage to your car, please be certain that it's for property damage only. When endorsing the check, please be certain to write those words above your signature. Also, read the release you are signing pertaining to any property damage loss. The language should be clear that you are not giving up any rights to pursue a personal injury claim. Do not trust the advice of the adjuster. Written words on a release take precedence over promises made by an insurance adjuster.

Under no circumstances should you ever file a small claims suit to collect for property damage or any other expenses.

In New Jersey there is a rule called the "Entire Controversy Doctrine." This means that you can bring only one lawsuit per dispute or event. So if you bring a lawsuit in small claims court and settle the case, you cannot file a second lawsuit for personal injuries. By filing a lawsuit for property damage on your own, you may lose your right to bring a claim for your personal injuries or financial losses by giving the insurance company a gift called the "Entire Controversy Doctrine."

SUMMARY

RULE: DO NOT DISPOSE OF OR REPAIR YOUR CAR WITHOUT HAVING THE AT-FAULT DRIVER'S INSURANCE COMPANY EVALUATE THE PROPERTY DAMAGE AND PROVIDE AN ESTIMATE OF REPAIR.

RULE: TAKE PLENTY OF PICTURES OF BOTH INTERNAL AND EXTERNAL PROPERTY DAMAGE TO YOUR CAR AND THE OTHER DRIVER'S CAR.

RULE: UNDER NO CIRCUMSTANCES SHOULD YOU EVER FILE A SMALL CLAIMS SUIT TO COLLECT FOR PROPERTY DAMAGE OR ANY OTHER EXPENSES.

RULE: IF YOU RECEIVE A CHECK FOR PROPERTY DAMAGE TO YOUR CAR, PLEASE BE CERTAIN THAT IT SAYS "FOR PROPERTY DAMAGE ONLY."

CHAPTER SEVEN

INSURANCE COVERAGE NJ NO-FAULT AUTOMOBILE INSURANCE

In New Jersey, there are two different insurance claims for injuries arising out of an automobile accident. One claim is against your own automobile insurance carrier and the other is against the person who caused the accident. Your own automobile insurance carrier will pay your medical bills and part of your lost wages. Your permanent losses, including your pain and suffering as well as your economic losses, would be the claim brought against both the driver who injured you and the insurance policy under which his or her car was insured. There will be further discussion about this separate and valuable claim later in this book.

New Jersey is part of a minority of states that have no-fault automobile insurance. This means that your own automobile insurance company will pay your medical bills and lost wages regardless of who or what caused your accident. For example, your own car insurance company would be responsible for your medical bills even if a car driven by a drunk driver, who was at the time smoking pot, rear-ended you while you were stopped at a red light. Under New Jersey no-fault law, the drunk driver would also be entitled to medical coverage and income continuation benefits under his or her own automobile insurance policy. Again, under no-fault insurance, fault does not matter for the payment of medical bills and lost wages.

As a trade-off for no-fault insurance, evidence of the amount paid for your medical bills cannot be used as evidence in a lawsuit brought against the person who caused your accident.

For all automobile accidents involving injuries, it is absolutely necessary for you to immediately apply for "personal injury protection" (PIP) medical and economic benefits through your own automobile insurance carrier. If you do not own a car but you live with a relative who owns a car, that relative's auto insurance carrier will be responsible for your medical bills and lost wages. The relative's insurance rates should not go up because you made a claim against the policy. It may be difficult to explain that concept to the relative, but that is the law and there is no way around it. In fact, by trying to protect the relative, you may be committing insurance fraud. As a result, it is absolutely necessary for you to report the accident to that insurance carrier and open a claim for PIP benefits.

If you were involved in an accident as a pedestrian and you had no car insurance of your own, then you would be entitled to PIP benefits from a New Jersey state agency called the Property Liability Insurance Guaranty Association, or PLIGA. Your lawyer would also need to make an application to PLIGA[4] if the driver who caused the accident had no automobile insurance.

Since your application for PIP benefits can be subpoenaed during the case, be sure to list all of your accident-related injuries.

New Jersey no-fault insurance will be responsible for your medical bills, including costs of medications, up to the amount of no-fault insurance purchased. Generally, there is $250,000 of medical expense coverage; however, you may have lower PIP coverage depending on your insurance policy. Please note that most often, there is a deductible of at least $250 per accident to be divided by all injured claimants. Beyond that, there generally is a copayment of twenty percent applicable to the first $5,000 in medical bills. If

---

4   Claims being brought for PLIGA benefits are subject to the strict statutory time limitations of NJSA 39:6-65 requiring that special written notice of a claim be filed within 180 days from the accident date. For the necessary forms, see: http://www.njguaranty.org.

you are denied medical treatment or are notified that your insurance carrier is refusing to pay your medical bills, it will be necessary for your lawyer to file a "PIP Suit" and make your PIP carrier pay the medical bills plus any legal fees you incurred because of their wrongful nonpayment of your medical bills. If you have met all of the conditions of your insurance policy, your lawyers will sue your insurance company if they refuse to pay for your reasonable and necessary medical treatment. Your treating doctors also have the right to bring their own arbitration against your insurance company should they not be paid for their outstanding medical bills incurred by you.

Because of the deductible and copayment requirements contained in your auto insurance policy, you may at the end of the case owe $1,250 or more, depending upon the deductible to which you are subject. If you have other medical coverage, such as major medical, such as Horizon Blue Cross Blue Shield of New Jersey, you can submit these unpaid deductibles and copayments to your regular health insurance company for them to pay. Unfortunately, these unpaid deductibles and copayments may again be subject to your health insurance company's normal deductibles.

It is important for you to know that PIP is responsible for paying all medical bills even if you had a pre-existing medical condition that the accident may have aggravated. PIP will also pay for psychiatric or psychological medical services for emotional conditions the accident causes or aggravates.

You should consult with your lawyer about questions you may have regarding the completion of your PIP application. For example, a skilled lawyer, already retained by you, should confidentially assist you in answering the specific questions as to how the accident happened, the nature and extent of your injuries, as well as questions pertaining to your lost wages.

Once your PIP application has been processed, or even at the time of your initial phone call to your PIP insurance carrier, you will receive a PIP claim number. It is extremely important that you notify the hospital billing office of this PIP claim number. It is also important to give it to all of your treating doctors. This will avoid future outstanding balances for which you may be responsible. You should notify your lawyers about medical bills that have been processed through any insurance carrier other than your PIP carrier for anything other than copayments or deductibles.

Three additional types of PIP benefits are allowable. First, each policy contains a benefit known as "essential services." Most PIP insurance policies provide for benefits of $12 per day to reimburse you for the costs you incur to have someone help you with your ordinary chores. This could include a housekeeper, landscaper, or a special driver. For example, if you hired someone part-time to clean your house every day for a week, you could submit a bill for $84 for reimbursement for that week's essential services.

Second, PIP will provide limited benefits for lost wages, which will be discussed later in this book. Third, a minimal funeral expense benefit allows a small sum toward the cost of a funeral.

New Jersey is a compulsory insurance state, which means it requires all drivers to operate insured vehicles. At one time, all drivers had to maintain at least $15,000 of "liability" coverage. However, that minimum no longer applies and some drivers who elected the basic policy have only PIP coverage and zero liability coverage. Other drivers have more than adequate coverage, such as up to $500,000 or more.

For example, a $500,000 insurance policy can be either a single limit policy that caps all claims at $500,000 or a split limit policy of $250,000/$500,000 that caps any single claim at $250,000 and all total claims at $500,000. Even more insurance coverage is available if a driver has an "umbrella policy," also called an excess liability policy.

It is quite common for a person to be involved in an accident with someone who is uninsured or has $15,000 or less in available insurance coverage. Under such circumstances, we look again at the injured driver's automobile insurance policy to determine whether there is additional "uninsured motorist coverage" (UM coverage), where the defendant is uninsured, or "underinsured motorist coverage" (UIM insurance), for situations where insurance coverage is insufficient.

UM and UIM insurance are different types of insurance that you purchased as part of your auto insurance policy or was part of the insurance attached to the car you were in at the time of the accident.

If the negligent driver is uninsured, you can make a claim against your own insurance company up to the UM limits you purchased. Your insurance company will then act as if they insure the wrongdoer. Your UM insurance carrier will either pay the claim or defend it through arbitration or trial.

The same applies to UIM coverage. If the negligent driver had insufficient insurance coverage to "make you whole" for all of your losses, you can make a claim against your insurance company up to the amount of the coverage you purchased minus the amount you collected from the negligent driver's insurance company.

If the person who caused the accident had minimum insurance coverage and you intend to make a claim for underinsurance benefits through your own insurance carrier, please note that you will need their written consent to settle with the negligent driver.

It can become extremely complicated when determining coverage among all of the available insurance policies. One should never attempt to settle this type of case on their own.

SUMMARY

RULE: YOUR OWN AUTO INSURANCE CARRIER WILL PAY YOUR MEDICAL BILLS AND PART OF YOUR LOST WAGES.

RULE: IT IS NECESSARY FOR YOU TO IMMEDIATELY APPLY FOR PERSONAL INJURY PROTECTION (PIP) MEDICAL AND ECONOMIC BENEFITS THROUGH YOUR OWN AUTOMOBILE INSURANCE CARRIER.

RULE: IF YOU WERE AN UNISURED PEDESTRIAN AT THE TIME OF THE ACCIDENT, YOU MUST APPLY FOR PIP BENEFITS FROM PLIGA.

RULE: IF THE NEGLIGENT DRIVER IS UNINSURED OR UNDERINSURED, YOU CAN MAKE A CLAIM AGAINST YOUR OWN INSURANCE POLICY FOR UP TO THE ADDITIONAL UM OR UIM BENEFITS YOU PURCHASED.

CHAPTER EIGHT

OTHER MEDICAL INSURANCE COVERAGE

If a portion of your accident-related medical bills, such as the deductibles or copayments, are paid by Medicare, Medicaid, workers' compensation insurance, or through an *ERISA* medical plan that your or your spouse's employer provides, please be aware that they too will need to be repaid out of your settlement for any money they paid on your behalf. The amount you need to repay will be part of the damages that your lawyers will claim on your behalf. It is important not to ignore any letters you receive from an employer-sponsored insurance company.

Most doctors and medical providers are aware of the financial hardship caused by an accident. As a result, they may be willing to wait until the end of your case for their payments, which may include outstanding deductibles and copayments. If they are willing to extend that courtesy, they will ask that you give them a "lien" on your settlement for their unpaid medical bills. You must sign the lien, which will be paid out of your final settlement. Even though a medical provider may be willing to wait for payment, please understand that their balance is not contingent upon the final outcome of the case. It's also important to notify your lawyer about any liens you have signed or are planning to sign.

If any bills are paid under an employer-sponsored plan and your employer or union is asserting a right of repayment, it will be necessary for them to prove that they are a "qualified ERISA plan." Your attorneys should make this complex legal analysis.

SUMMARY

RULE: ANY PAYMENTS FOR MEDICAL BILLS MADE BY MEDICARE, MEDICAID, WORKERS' COMPENSATION INSURANCE, OR A QUALIFIED ERISA MEDICAL PLAN WILL BE REPAID FROM YOUR SETTLEMENT.

RULE: UNDER CERTAIN CIRCUMSTANCES, MEDICAL PROVIDERS WILL ACCEPT A LIEN ON YOUR FILE AND WAIT FOR PAYMENT UNTIL THE CONCLUSION OF YOUR CASE.

CHAPTER NINE

INABILITY TO WORK
AND LOST WAGES

If injuries you sustained in a car accident prevent you from working, you must apply for any available union benefits or state disability benefits after waiting one week from the accident date. You may need to do this before you can get PIP income continuation benefits. If you are denied union or state disability payments, you may apply to your PIP insurance carrier for income continuation benefits. Under certain insurance policies, a person may collect for up to fifty-two weeks a minimum of $100 per week toward lost wages. If you bought higher PIP coverage at the time you purchased auto insurance, you may be entitled to collect up to $700 per week for income continuation benefits.

Please be careful of any comments you make to your employer, as an attorney can subpoena portions of their records and use them to undermine your case. Likewise, you need to tell your lawyers if you believe that your employment records may include references to any past injuries as well as whether you had to undergo a physical exam in order to get your job. Sometimes the findings of those physical exams can be either helpful or harmful to your case and therefore it is important to discuss this matter with your lawyers.

If you were self-employed at the time of the accident, it may be necessary for you to provide your income tax returns to the PIP insurance adjuster to document the income you allegedly lost. This can become extremely complicated, especially during challenging economic times, when you may be receiving income from your business but your business is still showing a loss. Under such circumstances, your lawyer needs to consult with your accountant to make the appropriate wage loss claim and to obtain PIP benefits.

SUMMARY

RULE: PIP WILL PROVIDE INCOME CONTINUATION BENEFITS UP TO THE AMOUNT OF COVERAGE PUR-CHASED. APPLICANTS MAY NEED TO FIRST APPLY FOR UNION OR STATE DISABILITY BENEFITS.

RULE: KEEP A DIARY OF ALL DATES YOUR ACCIDENT-RELATED INJURIES CAUSED YOU TO MISS WORK.

CHAPTER TEN

DOCUMENTING YOUR LOSSES

Many people think that a personal injury lawsuit is just about the injuries suffered. There is partial truth in that statement but a personal injury case is really about the harms and losses you and your family have suffered because of the accident.

These harms and losses are what we lawyers call "damages." Your damages include your pain and suffering, property damage losses, out-of-pocket expenses (including car rentals), lost income or lost income opportunities, your inconvenience, and the value of the loss of your recreational activities in which you can no longer participate. These activities can include your inability to play sports, dance, travel, exercise, play musical instruments, garden, or whatever was your passion. Even if you can still do those activities but you do so with pain, that loss is part of your overall damages.

Claims for damages may resolve out of court in the claims stage by a pre-lawsuit settlement. There may be reasons to settle pre-suit, but claims that settle prior to a lawsuit are often settled at lower dollar values.

In order to remember your harms and losses, keep a written journal of your injuries, doctor visits, daily pain, and your financial losses. Try to include in that journal an explanation of activities in which you were unable to participate. If you have a lawyer, keep these notes at his or her direction to protect them from the eyes of the insurance company lawyers by reason of "attorney-client privilege." Prudent lawyers provide clients with a special privilege notebook for their use. You can use your personal notebook as a reference to refresh your memory later.

Keep a list of all people who can testify to your pain and suffering as well as your inability to participate in your regular activities. These people may be called upon as witnesses should your case go to trial. Examples of these witnesses include family members, close friends, your spouse or children, co-workers, clergy, friends from gyms, dance partners, etc.

Make a note of anyone who may have witnessed your accident. There are eyewitnesses to the actual accident as well as eyewitnesses to the accident scene. Eyewitnesses to the accident scene include police officers, EMTs, ambulance drivers, tow operators, etc.

If representatives of the at-fault driver (e.g., an insurance adjuster) contact you, do not under any circumstances answer any questions or offer any information without consulting with an attorney. If a lawyer represents you, explain that you have a lawyer and refer their questions to your lawyer.

If your case goes to trial, other good witnesses may include physical therapists, chiropractors, radiologists, your primary care physician, and your treating physicians.

Your treating doctors would testify on your behalf as a fact witness regarding their physical findings and procedures performed. They may also act as expert witnesses and give opinion testimony as to causation or the relationship between the injuries and the accident as well as their opinion as to your future prognosis and permanency of the injuries. In such capacity, medical professionals often require thousands of dollars to appear in court, or attend depositions since they often cancel a full morning or afternoon of patients.

SUMMARY

RULE: A PERSONAL INJURY CASE IS REALLY ABOUT THE HARMS AND LOSSES A PERSON AND HIS OR HER FAMILY HAVE SUFFERED BECAUSE OF THE ACCIDENT.

RULE: KEEP A LIST OF ALL PEOPLE WHO CAN TES-TIFY AS TO YOUR PAIN AND SUFFERING AS WELL AS YOUR INABILITY TO PARTICIPATE IN YOUR REGU-LAR ACTIVITIES.

RULE: DO NOT ANSWER ANY QUESTIONS FROM ANY REPRESENTATIVE OF THE AT-FAULT DRIVER WITHOUT CONSULTING YOUR LAWYER.

CHAPTER ELEVEN

THRESHOLDS

In New Jersey, drivers who purchase automobile insurance have a choice of purchasing policies with either a "threshold" or "no threshold."[5] A threshold determines whether an accident victim can sue for non-permanent soft tissue injuries. If you selected a threshold, you may have saved money but in the process, you also may have unknowingly limited your right, and the right of resident relatives of your household, to bring a claim or lawsuit for accident-related injuries and damages.

Unless the person causing your accident was driving a commercial vehicle such as a truck or bus, you may be subject to a "threshold." However, if you purchased insurance with no threshold or a zero threshold, you will be entitled to bring a claim for both permanent and non-permanent injuries.

If you were involved in an accident that a commercial vehicle caused, such as a truck, you will not be subject to a threshold and you will be automatically deemed as a zero threshold case.[6]

The good news is that the law provides several exceptions that will "break" or "pierce" the threshold. An experienced and skilled lawyer can usually determine quite quickly whether a specific

---

5   Some insurance carriers will refer to a threshold as a "limitation on lawsuit option" or "verbal threshold," which restricts a person's right to sue for non-permanent soft tissue injuries. In comparison, a "zero threshold," also known as a "no limitation" threshold, gives a person an unlimited right to sue for any injuries.

6   Insurance companies not writing automobile insurance policies in New Jersey do not get the benefit of using the limitation on lawsuit threshold as a defense; as a result, persons injured by such out-of-state-insured vehicles are automatically subjected to no threshold.

exception applies. Through the years, hundreds of cases have been reported and serve as precedent for determining which injuries and conditions will successfully break the threshold.

If you selected or are subject to the "lawsuit threshold" ("verbal threshold" or "limitation on lawsuit threshold"), special language by your physician is required to "break" the threshold. That's why you will hear the threshold being referred to as the verbal threshold. You will be entitled to make a claim for all injuries, whether they are permanent or not, if any one single injury you suffered breaks the threshold and qualifies as a permanent injury.

As a rule, a person who is subject to a threshold cannot bring a lawsuit for pain and suffering unless he or she falls under any one of the following exceptions:[7] (1) a bodily injury that results in death; (2) dismemberment; (3) significant disfigurement or significant scarring; (4) displaced fractures; (5) loss of a fetus; (6) or a permanent injury within a reasonable degree of medical probability, other than scarring or disfigurement. An injury shall be considered permanent when the body part or organ, or both, has not healed to function normally and will not heal to function normally with further medical treatment.[8]

A ruptured disc or a herniated disc caused by a car accident generally will break the threshold. Also, it is important to know that if any one particular injury breaks a threshold, then a defendant will be responsible for all injuries, including those that would not on their own have broken the threshold.

In order to "break" the threshold, a physician must use special language in a medical narrative report that explains why a client's injuries are permanent. It is the use of certain language that "breaks" the threshold.

---

7   See Appendix F for full text of NJSA 39:6A-8

8   See NJSA 39:6A-8a.

Again, it's important to understand that if the vehicle that caused the accident was a commercial vehicle, such as a truck or bus, then in most instances it does not matter what threshold you had since you would be deemed to be an automatic zero threshold case.

In order to go forward with a lawsuit for threshold injuries, it will be necessary for your attorney to have your treating doctor sign a "Certification of Permanency" to be filed with the court. For that reason, the selection of your physician is extremely important for both medical and legal reasons. Do not hesitate to discuss this important issue further with your attorney.

SUMMARY

RULE: YOUR SELECTION OF A THRESHOLD IS AN IMPORTANT DECISION. IF FINANCIALLY POSSIBLE, ONE SHOULD PURCHASE THE ZERO THRESHOLD OPTION.

RULE: ACCIDENTS CAUSED BY COMMERCIAL VEHICLES ARE NOT SUBJECT TO A THRESHOLD, AND ARE AUTOMATICALLY DEEMED ZERO THRESHOLD CASES.

RULE: A PERSON WHO IS SUBJECT TO A THRESHOLD CANNOT BRING A LAWSUIT FOR PAIN AND SUFFERING UNLESS HE OR SHE FALLS WITHIN ANY ONE OF THE SIX EXCEPTIONS. ONE SHOULD CONSULT WITH A SKILLED PERSONAL INJURY LAWYER TO MAKE THAT DETERMINATION.

CHAPTER TWELVE

INJURIES AND MEDICAL TREATMENT

Your selection of treating doctors is an important decision that affects the success of your case. Quite often, clients unknowingly select physicians who are unwilling to cooperate with lawyers. If a physician refers you to a specialist, you should discuss the referral with your lawyer before you visit the specialist. Many doctors or other medical providers do not understand the technical requirements of the New Jersey Courts, which include specific language required in expert reports, nor do many of them understand or appreciate the importance of their availability to testify on your behalf at a court hearing.

You need to tell your treating doctors about all of your injuries and the amount and frequency of your pain.

You need to disclose to your treating doctors whether you suffered from any prior medical problem in the area of your injuries. Prior accidents and injuries are not necessarily harmful to your case. Your lawyer will need to know if you ever had any type of prior MRI or CT scans of your neck or back. Disclose this information to your lawyers as well as your medical doctors.

Under the current law in New Jersey, in certain circumstances a pre-existing unknown injury or medical condition, if aggravated by the accident, may actually add more value to your case. Here's what a judge tells a jury, word for word, about prior medical conditions, prior injuries or prior claims in the court's jury charge right before the jury deliberates:

I will now explain what happens if [plaintiff] had a predisposition or weakness which was causing no symptoms or
problems before the accident but made him/her more susceptible to the kind of medical problems he/she claims in
this case. If the injuries sustained in this accident combined
with that predisposition to create the plaintiff's medical
condition, then plaintiff is entitled to recover for all of
the damage sustained due to that condition. You must not
speculate that an individual without such predisposition or
latent condition would have experienced less pain, suffering, disability and impairment.[9]

In order to properly document and help prove an internal injury, take photographs of any scars, bruises, or abrasions as soon
as visible. Often these valuable photographs serve as evidence that
a particular body part sustained injury because of the accident. If
you undergo any surgery, you need to take photos of the incisions
after the bandages are removed.

Be certain not to miss any scheduled medical appointments or
physical therapy. Missed appointments or sporadic medical treatment creates a presumption that your injuries were minimal or, even
worse, insignificant.

If you are subject to a threshold, you must prove that you suffered a permanent injury by an "objective" test. You cannot prove
the permanency and true extent of your injuries without MRI or
CT scan studies. If you go for an MRI or CT scan, you should ask
for an extra copy of the images. They may give them to you in the
form of film sheets or on a CD ROM, which you can use as part

9   NJ Model Jury Charge 8.11F. See Appendix C for the full extent of
the Jury Charge and the application of the law pertaining to aggravation of
preexisting known conditions.

of your case. Do not tell them that you need this information for your lawyers. If you had any past MRI or CT studies done of the same body parts, try to recall where and when you had these tests done. If you cannot remember, give your lawyer as many details as possible about the prior testing to help locate your prior films.

If a doctor prescribes any medications, you should keep all of your prescription bottles as evidence of your use of prescription medications. Do not have the bottles refilled; instead order a new prescription by telephone and save that bottle as well. If it is necessary for you to go for epidural injections, your lawyer should arrange to ask the pain management physician to video record the procedure. You should give your lawyer plenty of notice before the procedure in order for him or her to arrange to send a videographer to record the procedure.

If you suffered a fracture due to the accident, your lawyers will again need those plain X-ray films so that their medical illustrators can make colorized copies of your fractures. Remember that a non-displaced (unseparated) fracture generally will not break the threshold; however, a displaced fracture will automatically break the threshold. You should get copies of those films from your doctor or give your lawyers the name of the custodian of those films so that they can obtain copies of them.

If you required surgery to implant screws, pins, or plates to stabilize your fracture and at some later date such medical hardware is removed, you should ask your surgeon to save the hardware and give it to you to hold as evidence as part of your case. Be sure to let your lawyers know that you have that hardware in your possession.

Unfortunately, from time to time, people suffer a second accident or injury after they retain lawyers. If that happens, you will need to notify your lawyers immediately of the event and discuss the effect of a subsequent accident upon your claim.

SUMMARY

RULE: THE SELECTION OF TREATING DOCTORS IS AN IMPORTANT DECISION THAT AFFECTS THE SUCCESS OF YOUR CASE.

RULE: DISCLOSE ALL PAST ACCIDENTS AND PAST INJURIES OR MEDICAL CONDITIONS TO YOUR DOCTORS AND LAWYERS.

CHAPTER THIRTEEN

ABOUT PAST ACCIDENTS, PRE-EXISTING CONDITIONS, OTHER INJURIES, AND CLAIMS

Insurance companies are becoming quite shrewd in investigating personal injury claims. The insurance industry keeps records of all accidents and the first thing they do is check you out for any past insurance claims of any nature. Again, be certain that you have told your lawyers about any past claims you may have made. Be aware that they may hire an investigator to follow you to observe your activities at any time to discredit or attack your credibility. In fact, they may even video record your physical activities for use later.

You need to advise your attorneys about any past accidents of any nature as well as past insurance claims. Insurance companies subscribe to services from the Central Index Bureau. This company collects claims information from all insurance companies and keeps detailed histories of any claims made by any person. As a subscriber of this service, the insurance company will certainly be aware of any accidents or claims you may have made in the past.

Under certain circumstances, it may be a good idea to gather past medical records in order to prove that the accident caused new injuries or show that the recent accident aggravated old injuries or pre-existing medical conditions.

Your lawyers will also need to know about any past or contemplated bankruptcies, past criminal convictions, unpaid child support, and a separation or divorce from a spouse. If given enough notice of your past problems, your lawyers may be able to eliminate or limit the harm such circumstances can cause to your case.

SUMMARY

RULE: DO NOT TRY TO CONCEAL ANY PAST CLAIMS OR PRIOR INJURIES SINCE THE INSURANCE INDUSTRY KEEPS RECORDS OF ALL OF YOUR PAST CLAIMS.

RULE: BE SURE TO TELL YOUR LAWYER ABOUT ANY PAST OR CONTEMPLATED BANKRUPTCIES, PAST CRIMINAL CONVICTIONS, UNPAID CHILD SUPPORT, AND DIVORCE OR SEPARATION FROM A SPOUSE.

CHAPTER FOURTEEN

YOUR ONLINE PROFILE AND LIFE

Many of our clients have decided to make much of their lives public by posting information and pictures on Facebook, MySpace, LinkedIn or other social media. You need to know that many good cases are being lost because of information contained on those pages. Insurance companies, their lawyers, and investigators are now making a habit of visiting those Web sites to obtain valuable information to use against you later. We urge you to use extreme caution in posting anything showing physical activity on your part.

However, this evidence may be extremely helpful if your cyber life shows how active you were prior to the accident. You may want to point this out to your lawyer and show him or her your pages.

Many of these online services now offer enhanced privacy settings. This will not be sufficient protection since a shrewd defense attorney can easily obtain a court order forcing you to produce your social media sites for inspection. After examining your home page, the attorney can even subpoena your online friends for their depositions.

In the past, insurance companies would hire expensive investigators to follow accident claimants and take videos or photographs of them engaging in physical activities that they claimed they were no longer able to perform. You need to make the decision that you will not provide this damaging evidence to the insurance company investigators by making harmful cyber comments and posts.

Be aware that you will be cyber stalked, and that a clever defense attorney will undoubtedly use damaging evidence to defeat your case.

SUMMARY

RULE: ANYTHING YOU PUT ONLINE, INCLUDING PHOTOS, CAN BE USED TO DISCREDIT YOU.

CHAPTER FIFTEEN

BORROWING MONEY AGAINST YOUR CASE

From time to time, you may hear advertisements about borrowing money against your pending case. We urge you not to get involved in these schemes. The interest rate charged by these companies is extremely high and may result in them having an interest in most of your settlement. We cannot overemphasize the damage that these lending companies can do to a case.

If you need money, you should consider exploring alternatives, such as borrowing from friends, landlords, or relatives. If you do, you should document the loan and let your lawyer know about it so that he or she can name the lender as a witness if necessary.

You should not ask your lawyer for a personal loan. Although your lawyer may desperately want to help you with a direct loan, he or she cannot. A lawyer's hands are tied by the strict ethics rules governing the practice of law.[10] The lending of money to a client is unethical and may result in the lawyer losing his or her license to practice law.

If a lawyer offers you any money to get you to hire him or her, you need to avoid that lawyer because he or she is crooked. You also need to know that many times these crooked lawyers will pay others to get you to hire them. These crooked lawyers may employ and pay people who are strangers to contact you, hoping to convince you to sign up with a particular lawyer. These strangers are called "runners." These runners often will visit accident victims in their homes or hospital rooms to try to solicit their business for a crooked lawyer. It is important for you to know that what they do

10   See Rule of Professional Conduct RPC 1:8(e).

is illegal. These runners are not recommending a particular lawyer to you for his or her great legal achievements. Instead, they are making their referrals for cash in their pockets. Stay far away from these people and report them to the local bar association.

Fortunately, for the legal profession, few lawyers engage in this type of unethical conduct. Avoid lawyers who do. An honest lawyer with a good reputation generally has no need or desire to illegally solicit cases.

You should also be skeptical of any direct solicitations you may receive by mail after an accident. Although many of these lawyers make themselves out to be trial lawyers, they may have little or no courtroom experience and are interested only in making a quick buck.

Often, people who have had positive legal experiences will refer a lawyer as an act of gratitude to the lawyer and friendship to you. Regardless, you still need to do your own independent research to make sure you find the right lawyer for your case.

SUMMARY

RULE: PERSONAL INJURY LAWYERS ARE ETHICALLY FORBIDDEN FROM LENDING MONEY TO THEIR CLIENTS.

RULE: IF AT ALL POSSSIBLE, DO NOT BORROW MONEY FROM A COMPANY OFFERING A LOAN AGAINST YOUR CASE.

RULE: BEWARE OF STRANGERS WHO SOLICIT THE SERVICES OF LAWYERS, AND ALWAYS DO YOUR OWN RESEARCH BEFORE DECIDING ON THE RIGHT LAWYER FOR YOUR CASE.

CHAPTER SIXTEEN

OTHER CONSIDERATIONS

Under no circumstances should you file for protection from your creditors under the bankruptcy laws without consulting first with your lawyers. If you file for protection under the bankruptcy laws, your case may become the property of your creditors or the appointed U.S. trustee. In fact, if you do not tell the U.S. trustee about your pending claim, you may be committing fraud upon the U.S. trustee as well as your creditors. Often, a skilled lawyer can establish a relationship with the trustee and negotiate a full or partial exemption. This can be done only with full advance disclosure to the trustee.

All states and even the federal government have different rules as far as how long someone has to bring a lawsuit. The time limit to bring a lawsuit is called the "statute of limitations." Please note that in New Jersey there is a two-year statute of limitations to bring a lawsuit for most personal injuries caused by negligence. In order to file or bring a lawsuit, you must file a document called a "complaint" with the clerk of the Superior Court of New Jersey, together with the appropriate filing fee.

The complaint must set forth the names and addresses of the plaintiff and all defendants and must include the theory of liability as well as the allegations of negligence. Again, the technical requirements of filing a lawsuit can be quite complex; hopefully, by the time a lawsuit is necessary, you will have hired an experienced trial lawyer.

Although your lawyers should keep track of your statute of limitations date in at least three different ways, you should be encouraged to call your lawyers well before the second anniversary of your accident to confirm that they have, in fact, filed a lawsuit.

Also be aware that there is a two-year statute of limitations to sue your PIP insurance carrier for nonpayment of medical bills. If a PIP carrier made any payment of your medical bills, the time limit is two years from the last date of payment of the last bill. If the carrier never made any payment whatsoever then the statute of limitations is four years from the accident date.

If the person who caused your New Jersey accident was working for a "public entity" such as the State of New Jersey, any county government, any municipality, or any of their authorities such as the Department of Public Works, Board of Education, etc. you will be subject to the New Jersey Tort Claims Act.[11] Under such circumstances, you will need to put the specific governmental entity on notice of the accident and file your claim on their special forms within ninety days of the accident. Giving this mandatory notice is called giving the governmental entity "Torts Claim Notice." If you fail to do this necessary step properly, you will likely lose your right to bring a claim.

All of these issues can be extremely complex. Seek competent legal advice as soon as possible. For example, the time limit to give notice to the Port Authority is different from other governmental entities and if a case involves the Port Authority of New York and New Jersey, it may be subject to only a one-year statute of limitations date to file a lawsuit.

LIENS AGAINST YOUR CASE

You also need to be aware that other people, insurance companies, or governmental agencies may have a particular interest in

---

11   New Jersey Statutes Annotated: NJSA 59:1-1 to 12-3

your case. In fact, their interest is a financial interest and they act as a "lien" on your case. A lien is a financial obligation that must be repaid before you receive any money. If workers' compensation insurance, Medicare, Medicaid, or a qualified employer-sponsored insurance plan (ERISA) paid your medical bills, they require repayment from your portion of any settlement. Other liens that may apply are unpaid child support, certain welfare liens, and, under certain circumstances, payments made by your PIP carrier.

TAXES

The good news is that money received as a settlement regarding pain and suffering claims is not now taxable. Settlements paid in the future known as structured settlements are also generally not taxable if properly created and funded. However, this too can be complex, especially in employment cases, if a portion of the settlement is allocated as lost income.

INTEREST

Under certain circumstances, the court may award interest after a favorable jury verdict. The interest awarded is subject to both state and federal income tax laws.

If a case settles either out of court or at the time of trial, there is no interest because no judgment is entered against a defendant. Interest becomes a factor only if a judgment is entered because of a jury verdict. The official court rules set different interest rates for pre- and post-judgment interest.

SUMMARY

RULE: DO NOT FILE FOR BANKRUPTCY WHILE A PERSONAL INJURY CLAIM IS PENDING.

RULE: IN NEW JERSEY, THERE IS A TWO-YEAR STATUTE OF LIMITATIONS FOR AUTOMOBILE AND MOST TYPES OF PERSONAL INJURY CASES.

RULE: A TORTS CLAIM NOTICE MUST BE FILED WITHIN NINETY DAYS OF AN ACCIDENT IF THE NEGLIGENCE OF A GOVERNMENT WORKER OR AGENCY CAUSED IT.

RULE: PERSONAL INJURY AWARDS FOR PAIN AND SUFFERING ARE NOT SUBJECT TO TAXES.

RULE: MEDICAL BILLS PAID BY ERISA PLANS, MEDICARE, MEDICAID, AND UNPAID CHILD SUPPORT ARE LIENS ON A SETTLEMENT AND MUST BE PAID OUT OF ANY SETTLEMENT.

CHAPTER SEVENTEEN

INJURIES TO CHILDREN

Unfortunately, from time to time a child is injured because of the negligence of another. For the most part, the law treats children the same as adults with a few exceptions.

In New Jersey and most jurisdictions, children under the age of seven are considered incapable of being legally accountable for negligence. This also makes children legally incapable of being comparatively negligent if they are injured.

New Jersey is a jurisdiction where there is no immunity from lawsuits between family members. This means that family members such as a child or a spouse can sue any other family member for damages because of that family member's negligence. For example, if Mom drove a car off the road while Dad and child were passengers, Mom can be sued by the rest of her family for money damages. Mom would have no defense or immunity from being sued. Not only are these suits permitted, they are quite common.

Children are often injured in car accidents. They tend to be extremely resilient and bounce back quickly from injuries. In car crashes, younger children, or "children of tender years," are usually well protected by car seats and suffer no harm. If they suffer injuries, often they are fearful of medical treatment and, as a result, they do not complain about pain or discomfort.

The types of accidents common with children are bicycle accidents, trip and fall accidents, burn injuries, injuries from unsafe products, dog bites, swimming pool accidents, sport-related injuries, accidents while attending summer camp, injuries from other children, and injuries due to medical malpractice. Also long-term psychological injuries should not be overlooked.

The most devastating injuries are burn injuries. Such injuries can occur because of a household fire due to an adult's negligence, lack of smoke detectors or alarms, or lack of a safe exit. For example, a landlord is negligent if he or she puts bars or chicken wire over a window, blocking a safe exit from the home. Children can also suffer burns from hot liquids being spilled on them or from overheated bathtub water in violation of local ordinances.

Another common injury to children involves brain injuries. These injuries can occur either by an accident where a child suffers a serious concussion, or because of ingesting lead paint. Brain injuries are extremely complex and many times aren't detected until months or years after an injury occurs.

Since it is often difficult to accurately predicting the permanent nature of injuries to children, the statute of limitations applicable to children's cases in New Jersey is extended until two years from a child's eighteenth birthday, or up to the twentieth birthday.[12] However, for birth-related injuries resulting from a doctor or hospital's negligence, the statute of limitations for children born after July 1, 2004, is until their thirteenth birthday. Children born before July 1, 2004 (which is the date when the law was changed), still have until their twentieth birthday to file a lawsuit.

Under the current New Jersey law, children also benefit from a lower contingency fee if a case settles before the start of a trial. The normal contingency fee of 33 1/3 percent is reduced to

---

12   Another exception to the general rule that a minor has until his or her twentieth birthday to bring a personal injury claim involves a suit against a PIP carrier for nonpayment of medical bills. As a result, the statute of limitations will not be tolled and the minor will be subjected to the same rules as if he or she were an adult.

25 percent of a settlement. If a trial begins, the legal fee is the same as if the child were an adult.

Since a child is incapable of entering into a binding contract and may be too young to make appropriate long-term decisions, the law requires that a lawsuit involving a child be brought by an adult who acts as a "guardian ad litem." The guardian is usually one of the child's parents who is entitled to make all decisions for the child pertaining to the lawsuit. Any decisions made by the guardian must be in the best interest of the child.

Cases involving a child that settle either before or after trial are also treated differently. Since a child has until he or she is twenty years old to bring a lawsuit, our legal system makes certain that a child has received fair and just compensation and that a defendant who pays a claim will not be sued again by the child for the same injuries. In order to protect both parties, there is a special proceeding where a judge holds a hearing and determines if a settlement is fair under the circumstances as it relates to the cause of the accident and the injuries the child suffered. This special hearing is called a "friendly." A friendly hearing legitimizes a settlement called an "infant compromise."

At a friendly hearing, a judge hears testimony and reviews affidavits provided by physicians in order to arrive at a decision regarding the fairness of the settlement. The judge will also closely examine the final settlement's financial arrangements, including the fees and costs a lawyer will receive. At this hearing, parents can request approval for reimbursement of the monies they laid out or losses they incurred. However, the rest of the money is clearly the property of the "infant" (under the age of eighteen) child.

If the settlement involves periodic payments in the future, or what is known as a "structured settlement," the court will require additional testimony and evidence concerning the financial stability of the insurance company that will be responsible for making those future structured settlement payments.

Once a settlement is approved, the judge must order that all settlements in excess of $5,000 be held in a high interest-bearing account administered by the county Surrogate until that child turns eighteen, unless money is needed for that child's medical treatment or emergencies. When the child turns eighteen, he or she will be entitled to receive the full lump sum of their portion of the settlement together with all accumulated interest.

SUMMARY

RULE: SPECIAL RULES APPLY TO PERSONAL INJURY CASES REGARDING INJURED CHILDREN.

RULE: FOR NON-BIRTH-RELATED INJURIES, CHILDREN HAVE UNTIL THEIR TWENTIETH BIRTHDAY TO BRING A LAWSUIT.

RULE: A JUDGE IN A "FRIENDLY" HEARING MUST APPROVE ALL SETTLEMENTS REGARDING CHILDREN.

RULE: SETTLEMENTS INVOLVING CHILDREN ARE SUBJECT TO A 25 PERCENT CONTINGENCY FEE. THE SURROGATE COURT WILL HOLD A CHILD'S PORTION OF A SETTLEMENT IN AN INTEREST-BEARING ACCOUNT UNTIL THE CHILD'S EIGHTEENTH BIRTHDAY.

CHAPTER EIGHTEEN

HIRING THE RIGHT LAWYER

According to the Supreme Court of New Jersey, the hiring of an attorney is an important decision. Before making your choice of attorney, you should give this matter careful thought. In fact, in any direct solicitation letter a lawyer mails to a potential client, the Supreme Court of New Jersey requires the letter to prominently display the following exact language:

> Before making your choice of an attorney, you should give this matter careful thought. The selection of an attorney is an important decision. If this letter is inaccurate or misleading, report the same to the Committee of Attorney Advertising, Hughes Justice Complex, CN037, Trenton, N.J. 08625.

Not all lawyers have the necessary knowledge or experience to handle a personal injury claim. New Jersey does not permit lawyers to advertise themselves as "specialists." However, they may state their practice areas of concentration.

One important exception you need to know about dates back to 1980, when the Supreme Court of New Jersey created an exception to that rule with the certification of trial attorneys.

The reason you need to know about this is that you want to hire a lawyer who is certified or has the same trial experience as a *Certified Civil Trial Attorney.* In New Jersey, less than 3 percent of all licensed lawyers have become designated as Certified Civil Trial Attorneys. You need to know if your attorney is certified.

Not all states certify lawyers as civil trial attorneys. New York, for example, does not certify their attorneys and many highly qualified New Jersey lawyers have gained most of their trial experience in New York. Unless you know about your attorney's trial experience firsthand, hire only Certified Civil Trial Attorneys.

In order for a New Jersey lawyer to become a Certified Civil Trial Attorney, he or she must have practiced for a minimum of five years. The attorney must have tried at least ten jury trials and must have over thirty days of courtroom trial experience. All of the judges who may have presided over those trials as well as the adversary attorneys may be called upon to evaluate the applicant.[13]

The applicant attorney must have an unblemished reputation, undergo a new background check, and be free of ethics violations. The applicant attorney must also supply the names of individuals for recommendations and must further prove that he or she participated in a minimum of thirty credit hours of continuing legal education programs during the three-year period prior to applying for certification.

After the application is approved, the candidate must travel to Trenton to take a full-day written examination, parts of which analyze video courtroom depictions shown to the candidates. Only after passing the examination can a lawyer proudly designate him or herself as a Certified Civil Trial Attorney.

There are many lawyers qualified to try cases who never qualified for the exam or never took the test, but the consumer has no way of knowing that other than taking the attorney's word that he or she is qualified to try a case.

If your lawyer at one time handled your divorce or your real estate closing, he or she is probably not right for this case. Most qualified personal injury lawyers practice in groups as law firms

---

13   NJ Rules of Court R 1:39-1

that devote their entire resources to representing injured individuals. These types of lawyers understand the intricacies of the body of law commonly known as "tort law." They have experience with experts in the field and they have developed a good measure of respect from the insurance adjusters and their defense attorneys.

Although 95 percent of all cases settle at or before trial, you still need to hire a lawyer that has built his or her reputation in the courtroom. Insurance companies know which lawyers are certified and which lawyers will go the distance and try a case. They also know which lawyers will always take the easy way out and settle with minimum effort and expense. If an insurance company believes that your lawyer represents a threat to them in the courtroom, they will more than likely try to enter into a settlement that will be more favorable to you.

Here are some of the questions you need to ask your lawyers:

Q. What percentage of your practice involves representing injured people?

You can get a good idea about your lawyer's qualifications and commitment to the interests of injured claimants by his or her answer to this question. Generally, I believe that if more than half of an attorney's practice is devoted to representing plaintiffs, he or she may have sufficient knowledge to represent you. However, there are other factors to consider.

Also, lawyers who substantially work on a contingency fee basis have a need to move their cases along to get paid. You would not want your file to sit aside while your lawyer is engaged in doing a real estate closing or divorce.

Q. Are you or any members of your firm certified as a Civil Trial Attorney by the Supreme Court of New Jersey?

As discussed above, even if your prospective attorney answers that he or she is certified, you will still need to ask if he or she tried plaintiffs' personal injury cases as part of that certification process. Not all civil trials are personal injury cases. The attorney may have received trial certification litigating business disputes.

Q. Tell me about some of the last cases you or members of your firm have tried.

Again, if you want a good out-of-court settlement the insurance company needs to know that you mean business and have hired lawyers that pose a threat to them. Don't be afraid to ask about some of your law firm's past trials and results. The insurance companies surely will know this information so why shouldn't you know about your lawyer's track record?

Q. Have you ever handled a case like mine before?

This is a fair question. While most of a personal injury lawyer's practice will consist of motor vehicle accidents, not all personal injury lawyers have experience in handling workers' compensation claims, product liability claims, or medical malpractice claims. Some cases combine different aspects of "subspecialties" such as the Toyota sudden acceleration cases or the unfortunate situation where a person injured in a car accident goes on to become a victim of medical malpractice.

Q. Who, aside from you, will be working on my file?

The preparation of a personal injury case is a bit like a scavenger hunt. All relevant past and present medical records need to be collected and analyzed. Documents need to be continually submitted to opposing counsel. You don't want your lawyer directing his or her attention to collecting these volumes of documents. What you want is to be certain that a qualified lawyer has reviewed and analyzed all potential evidence to use either as part of your case or to anticipate its use by the defense in order to minimize its impact. Such evidence can include past personal injury claim files or past medical reports and records.

You will also want your lawyer to have sufficient backup coverage, in case of illness or a lengthy trial engagement, so that the resolution of your case will not be unreasonably delayed. By way of example, larger offices may have various legal teams responsible for each client's case. For strategic reasons, they may decide which qualified member of the legal team will handle certain aspects of a client's case. The entire team of lawyers may meet regularly to discuss various aspects of their client's case. Rather than delay a case they may arrange for a lawyer to cover an event such as an arbitration or deposition so that a client's case will move closer toward settlement or trial.

Q. Does your lawyer participate in continuing legal education offered by the New Jersey Association for Justice?

In New Jersey, all lawyers must attend twenty-four hours of continuing legal education every two years. No particular area of the law is required. The New Jersey Association for Justice provides continuing legal education with a concentration in the areas of interest to lawyers who represent the injured. While general practitioners will need to stay current in all areas of the law, personal injury lawyers will devote almost all of their hours staying current in the ever-changing area of personal injury law.

Q. Does your firm have the financial resources to advance all costs on my case and what will those costs be?

Generally, it is expensive to process a personal injury case. No case can go forward without an expert narrative report. Medical doctors generally charge between $500 and $1,000 for a medical report even on a routine case. Medical records, which also cost money, are insufficient alone to resolve a case since a plaintiff's lawyer requires a narrative report with the doctor's opinions regarding the cause of the injuries and the permanency of the injuries.

Cases involving catastrophic injuries require several other expert witnesses. Such other experts may include accident reconstructionists, life care planners, vocational rehabilitation experts, safety engineers, and economists.

These nonmedical expert witnesses often act as consultants early on in the case. They often conduct their own investigation and do their own research. Later, opposing counsel will often take their oral depositions. They receive hourly compensation for their efforts. Expert witnesses can be quite costly, but in order to prove certain parts of a case an expert witness is required. For this reason, you need to know that your lawyer will carefully select your expert witnesses and have the financial resources to promptly pay their bills.

Once a case is put into suit, additional expenses will be required, consisting of court filing fees, deposition costs, and trial costs. You need to know that your lawyer will advance all of these costs and that cash flow issues will not delay your case.

Keep in mind, any litigation costs advanced by a lawyer will be deducted from the gross settlement amount before his or her legal fee is computed. What that means is that in the end, the lawyer is actually going to be paying for one-third of the disbursements since his or her fee will be reduced by that amount.[14]

---

14 For example, if a case settles for ten dollars and your lawyer advanced one dollar, the legal fee will be one-third of nine dollars, not ten. The law firm will be reimbursed for the dollar advanced but that will ultimately reduce his or her fee by thirty-three cents. Your lawyer will at the time of distribution receive back his dollar plus a three dollar fee.

Q. Will you accept my case on a contingency basis?

If you hire your lawyer on a contingency fee basis, he or she will receive a legal fee only if there is payment by reason of a settlement or collected judgment.[15] On a contingency basis, the lawyer will get a percentage of the amount collected. Generally, you should want your lawyer to accept your case on a contingency fee basis, especially if significant insurance is involved. If you retain a lawyer on an hourly basis, you will pay the monthly amount you are billed based on your lawyer's hourly rate and time committed to your file. You generally will pay a legal fee whether or not you win the case. You certainly can hire a personal injury lawyer on an hourly basis; however, under an hourly arrangement you will more than likely be required to give the lawyer an up-front cash retainer and advance all expenses and expert witness fees incurred as part of the claim. If a lawyer asks for an hourly fee arrangement, he or she probably has little confidence in winning the case.

If a lawyer accepts your case on a contingency basis, he or she will likely do whatever is necessary to move the case along as expeditiously as possible.

Q. What is your experience with the defendant's insurance company?

Active personal injury attorneys are aware of which insurance carriers will settle or force a case to trial. Insurance carriers consider numerous factors to determine whether they will deny payment on a claim. An experienced personal injury attorney generally utilizes a different case resolution strategy for each insurance carrier he or she goes up against. If your New Jersey defendant is insured by Allstate, State Farm, Geico, New Jersey Manufacturers (NJM), or Progressive, you better make sure your lawyer knows his or her way around the courtroom.

---

15   NJ Court Rule 1:21-7 codifies the maximum contingency fee that a lawyer can charge. For full text of the rule, see Appendix D.

Q. Have you been selected or honored for your accomplishments as an attorney?

Lawyers within their community recognize accomplished personal injury lawyers for their achievements. Martindale-Hubbell is an independent lawyer rating agency. The highest rating they can give to a lawyer or law firm is an "AV" rating.

Another group that rates lawyers is *Law and Politics Magazine*. Each year throughout America and in New Jersey, they poll lawyers to determine the top 5 percent of the practitioners in each area of the law. They recognize these lawyers as "SuperLawyers."[16]

Many accomplished lawyers will hold positions as an officer or trustee of a state bar association, trial lawyer association such as the New Jersey Association for Justice, (formerly the Association of Trial Lawyers of America-NJ), or a local county bar association. If your lawyer is an officer or serves on the board of governors of such an association, he or she probably has earned the respect of other lawyers within the practice area.

SUMMARY

RULE: BEFORE MAKING YOUR CHOICE OF AN ATTORNEY, YOU SHOULD GIVE THIS MATTER CAREFUL THOUGHT. THE SELECTION OF AN ATTORNEY IS AN IMPORTANT DECISION.

RULE: DON'T BE AFRAID TO ASK QUESTIONS ABOUT A LAWYER'S EXPERIENCE BEFORE MAKING YOUR SELECTION.

---

16   Required language by New Jersey Supreme Court decision pursuant to litigation regarding the constitutionality of Opinion 39 requires lawyers to state, "No aspect of this advertisement has been approved by the New Jersey Supreme Court."

CHAPTER NINETEEN

ABOUT LEGAL FEES

In order to establish an attorney-client relationship to make a claim for your damages, it will be necessary for you to hire an attorney.

The lawyer you will hire will represent you in connection with suing the at-fault driver for your damages. As discussed, these damages include your pain and suffering as well as your economic damages. It is important to know that a lawyer cannot charge you a legal fee on payments made by the PIP carrier for medical bills and lost wages under income continuation plans. Even if your lawyer sues the PIP carrier to force payment, the losing insurance carrier will pay those legal bills, not you. Most personal injury lawyers also do not charge a legal fee on the property damage portion of your claim.

You hire a lawyer by entering into a written agreement, which is a *retainer agreement*. This agreement also authorizes the lawyer to act on your behalf and sets forth how you will pay the lawyer. If you hire a lawyer on an hourly basis, you will pay an up-front cash payment. Under an hourly retainer, you will pay your lawyer whether the case is won or lost.

Another way of hiring a lawyer is on a contingency basis. This is called a contingent fee arrangement under New Jersey Court Rule 1:21-7. This means that you will be responsible to pay your lawyer a legal fee only if there is a financial recovery.

The same court rule is used to set the percentage a lawyer can legally charge for a New Jersey matter. That fee starts at 33 1/3 percent and is adjusted automatically to a lesser fee for portions of a recovery over $500,000. The rule also requires that a contingency fee in cases involving minors below the age of eighteen not exceed 25 percent if the case is settled prior to trial.

When you retain a lawyer on a contingent fee basis, the lawyer will likely advance all expenses and disbursements for court costs and expert reports. At the end of your case, you will reimburse the party who advanced the out-of-pocket lawsuit-related expenses before the legal fee is calculated. While a client will not be responsible for any legal fees if a case is lost at trial, the client may be responsible for out-of-pocket disbursements under a contingent fee arrangement. For that reason, a client should consider closely following the attorney's advice as to whether to settle a case before going to trial.

These issues and the costs associated with a trial should be discussed in detail with your attorney if your case is going to trial.

SUMMARY

RULE: NEW JERSEY COURT RULE 1:21-7 REGULATES THE PERCENTAGE CONTNINGENCY FEE A LAWYER CAN CHARGE.

CHAPTER TWENTY

WORKING WITH YOUR ATTORNEYS

Successful lawyers are extremely active in handling their clients' matters. They spend much of their time in court arguing or trying cases. As a result, it may be difficult to communicate with them. You should be encouraged to speak with your attorneys at any time. However, to avoid frustration and to get an immediate response, you should initially ask your questions to your case manager. Quite often, he or she will be able to provide you with a timely answer to your question right on the spot. A highly skilled case manager may have decades of experience in managing personal injury cases and his or her participation and input into your claim will certainly add value to your case.

If you do not hear from your lawyers for several months, do not assume that they are not working on your case. Quite often, their work is done behind the scene and they are busy securing all of the information necessary as part of your case. Under most circumstances, lawyers will not consider filing suit until all medical treatment has been completed.

If, however, you lose trust, or confidence in your lawyers, you are permitted to discharge them and hire new counsel. The new attorney who takes over your file will be responsible to pay out of his or her "contingent legal fee portion" an amount sufficient to fairly compensate the discharged lawyer for services until he or she was terminated.[17]

---

17   The portion of the legal fee paid to a discharged lawyer is based upon several factors including the amount of time spent working on a particular case, the stage of proceedings, and the amount of any offer received prior to

Discuss any problems you experience with a lawyer as soon as practicable. We urge you not to discharge a lawyer, since it is a drastic move on your part, unless you lose confidence in the lawyer or you no longer trust the lawyer's judgment.

If you are being represented by a larger firm and for some reason you are not satisfied with the lawyer handling your case, whether the lawyer is a partner or an associate, you should ask the managing partner to reassign your case to another lawyer within the firm.

Please understand that if a lawyer discusses with you the problematic aspects of your case, the lawyer is only doing his or her job. Do not interpret those necessary discussions as your lawyer being negative or "on their side." Lawyers receive specific training to analyze potential defenses and to affirmatively deal with those issues.

SUMMARY

RULE: COMMUNICATE OPENLY WITH YOUR LAWYER, ESPECIALLY IF YOU'VE LOST CONFIDENCE IN HIS OR HER COMMITMENT TO YOUR CASE.

RULE: YOU CAN DISMISS YOUR CURRENT LAWYERS IF YOU ARE DISSATISFIED WITH THEM. HIRING NEW LAWYERS WILL NOT INCREASE YOUR FINAL LEGAL FEE.

---

discharge. The fee paid to a discharged lawyer, assuming no legal malpractice was committed, should be a reasonable sum in relation to the services received and the final outcome of the case. This amount is known as "quantum merit." This determination is customarily negotiated between the lawyer taking over a particular case and the discharged lawyer. If the lawyers cannot agree, the courts will decide the allocation of the legal fee between the respective lawyers.

CHAPTER TWENTY-ONE

HOW LONG WILL YOUR CASE TAKE?

You may be wondering how long your case will take until it is resolved. Since each case is unique and there may be factors outside of your lawyer's control that can affect the timetable of a particular case, it is difficult to predict how long it will take. Most cases settle between twelve and thirty-six months from the time of your accident. For the most part, settlement negotiations do not start until medical treatment has finished. Only then can a doctor prepare a narrative report regarding a person's permanent injuries. Do not rush settlement negotiations, because early negotiations usually result in small settlement offers.

One of the factors that can delay a claim is the claim resolution policy of the defendant's insurance carrier. Some carriers, such as Allstate, Geico, and New Jersey Manufacturers, do not readily settle automobile accident cases that involve soft tissue injuries and are subject to the lawsuit threshold. Instead, they will force them to trial.

Other factors may involve other people injured in the same accident who are not willing to settle or abandon their claims. Occasionally, a defense attorney will drag out a case until jury selection before recommending a settlement to his or her carrier.

A common problem to be expected is that scheduling conflicts will tie up one of the lawyers involved in the trial or that there are just no available judges to preside over the trial due to previously assigned cases. The court will generally hold the case for a week or recycle it to set a new trial date. This can happen several times.

If your case goes to trial, you should be fully prepared in advance of the trial date. Cases can settle at any stage of trial, including jury selection. Quite often, insurance carriers will want to see if you are willing to show up for trial in order for them to enter into meaningful settlement negotiations.

If you do go the distance and obtain a successful jury verdict after a trial, the case could still drag on because of post-judgment motions, appeals, and even retrials. Nothing is guaranteed by the process.

SUMMARY

RULE: THERE ARE MANY FACTORS THAT CAN DELAY THE RESOULTION OF A CASE. HOWEVER, MOST CASES ARE RESOLVED BETWEEN TWELVE AND THIRTY-SIX MONTHS FROM THE TIME OF THE ACCIDENT.

RULE: BE PREPARED FOR SCHEDULING CONFLICTS AND DELAYS BEYOND YOUR LAWYERS' CONTROL.

CHAPTER TWENTY-TWO

WHAT'S YOUR CASE WORTH?

You may also be wondering what your case is worth. That is a fair question. However, experience shows that at the beginning stages, it is way too early to put a value on any case. Factors to consider include the nature and extent of any injury, out-of-pocket losses, prior medical conditions, your own actions that may have contributed to the accident, the amount of insurance coverage available, and even the county where the case will be filed. No reputable lawyer can put a value on a case until all of the facts from both sides are known. That being said, here are some of the factors to be considered:

1. The quality of the lawyer you hire.
2. The nature of the accident and whether there is any comparative[18] negligence on your part.
3. The nature and extent of your permanent injuries.
4. The threshold you selected and whether your injuries break that threshold.
5. The amount of available insurance coverage.
6. Your economic losses, including your past and future lost wages.

---

18   New Jersey is a comparative negligence state that requires a jury to determine the percentage of fault a plaintiff may have contributed to the cause of a particular accident. If a plaintiff is found to have caused more than 50 percent of the accident's negligence, he or she will be barred from a financial award. Any negligence found on the part of a plaintiff will also be deducted from any jury award by the same percentage of fault. Other states may be "contributory negligence" jurisdictions, which, under some state laws, may act as a complete bar to any financial recovery even if the plaintiff is found responsible for as little as one percent of the overall fault.

7. Your medical treatment. Surgery always increases the value of an injury.

8. The quality of the opinions of your treating doctors as well as their reputations and availability to testify on your behalf.

9. Whether you have any visible scars.

10. The nature and extent of your inability to engage in your usual, customary activities and recreational activities.

11. Whether future surgery is foreseeable.

12. The severity of the property damage to the cars involved in the collision.

13. The county in which your case can be brought, the demographic nature of the potential jurors in that county, as well as that county's jury verdict history.

14. Your ability to articulate yourself in a deposition or on the witness stand during a trial.

15. Whether you follow the guidance and instructions your lawyer gives you.

16. The amount of out-of-pocket liens to be repaid including ERISA liens, Medicare, Medicaid, and charity liens, and whether the amount of such liens is admissible into evidence at the time of trial.

17. Whether you have had past injuries or claims to the same body parts.

18. The quality and interpretation of your MRI films.

19. The judge assigned to your particular case and whether he or she has a bias to either plaintiffs or defendants.

20. The amount of time that has passed since your accident.

21. Your age and future economic losses.

22. Economic losses and loss of services suffered by your spouse.

23. The quality of the testimony of your lay witnesses, your friends, and family.
24. Whether the defendants continue to stay financially solvent and remain in business.

Since there are no books or charts to which a lawyer can refer in order to come up with a case value, it's basically experience and skill that determine the value of a case for settlement purposes.

A claim not to be overlooked involves the past, present and future hardship that an injury places on a spouse. For that reason, your husband or wife will be named as an additional plaintiff. This derivative claim, also known as a "per quod" claim, is for loss of consortium, society, and companionship and may include personal losses such as a loss of physical intimacy between the couple. Normally, if a case is settled, this case is merged into the entire settlement to the injured person. However, if the case goes to trial, the jury will be asked to award separate damages to the aggrieved spouse.

SUMMARY

RULE: THE VALUE OF A PERSONAL INJURY CASE IS HIGHLY COMPLEX, REQUIRING THE CONSIDERATION OF MANY FACTORS.

CHAPTER TWENTY-THREE

THE LITIGATION PROCESS

If a case cannot be settled during the claims stage, it will be necessary to file suit. All states and the federal government have different time limits to file a claim in the courts. In New Jersey, an injured person generally has two years from the date of the accident to file suit for bodily injuries caused by negligence.

As stated before, minors have two years from the age of eighteen to file suit, or until their twentieth birthday.[19] As mentioned earlier, the period of time in which a lawsuit must be filed is known as the "statute of limitations." In New Jersey, there is a six-year statute of limitations to file a suit for property damage losses. If a lawsuit is not filed within the appropriate statute of limitations, then the case will be dismissed against the wrongdoer and there will be no legal right for the injured person to proceed.[20]

Under certain circumstances in an automobile accident case, a permanency certificate signed by a physician should accompany the complaint. Medical malpractice cases require an Affidavit of Merit, signed by a physician stating that from his or her initial observation, it appears that malpractice may have been committed.

---

19   Birth-related injuries are subject to a separate statute of limitations for minors born after July 2004, which now requires lawsuits to be filed prior to age thirteen. For children born prior to July of 2004, the statute of limitations remains two years beyond the age of eighteen, or until age twenty.

20   For medical malpractice cases, there is a two-year discovery rule that, under certain circumstances, can extend the statute of limitations to two years from the date the injured knew or should have known that he or she suffered an injury due to medical negligence.

Although there is no law requiring a litigant to hire a lawyer in order to use the courts, it cannot be overemphasized what a critical mistake it would be to represent yourself instead of hiring a qualified lawyer. The litigation process is loaded with minefields and if you step on one of them, your case will be dismissed by the court.

A lawsuit is filed by preparing a document called a "complaint" and bringing it to the clerk of the court in the county where the suit is being filed. The county in which the lawsuit is filed is known as the "venue." The person on whose behalf the complaint is being filed is known as the plaintiff. The person or party who is being sued is known as the defendant. There are both legal and technical requirements that must be followed when drafting and filing a complaint. The complaint must set forth sufficient facts as well as the theories of negligence to state a "cause of action" against each defendant. The physical act of filing a complaint is accomplished by paying the filing fee of several hundred dollars and receiving back a copy of the document stamped "FILED" by the clerk of the court. The court will then assign a "docket number" to your complaint. According to the "New Jersey Rules of Courts," this complaint must be "served" together with a "summons" upon the defendant named in the complaint within a certain time limit; otherwise, the case will be dismissed.

Once the defendant is served with the summons and complaint he or she will have thirty days to file an answer setting forth denials and separate defenses. During this same period of time, the insurance company will appoint or hire a lawyer to represent the defendant. From this date forward, the parties to the lawsuit will have initially three hundred days to engage in "discovery."

The discovery process consists of drafting and serving your written interrogatory questions upon the defendant and responding to the defendant's uniform interrogatory questions. There are time limits involved that must be followed. Generally, after the written discovery stage is completed, both parties have the right to question and interview anyone under oath before a certified court stenographer in what is known as an "oral deposition" or "examination under oath."

Generally, clients and lawyers appear at depositions for both your statements and the defendant's statements under oath. It is a formal meeting that normally takes place in a lawyer's conference room. Clients should be fully prepared prior to submitting themselves to a deposition. Preparation for a deposition consists of reviewing your interrogatory answers as well as the defendant's interrogatory answers in order to understand the defense. You should be familiar with your medical history as well as the facts of your case. The purpose of a deposition is to "discover" facts, including those that could lead to other relevant evidence. Personal questions may be asked during a deposition for discovery purposes that would not ordinarily be allowed during a trial. You will be able to testify as to the impact of the injury on the quality of your life. You need to be prepared to list all of those activities you are no longer able to do because of the injuries you suffered.

Toward the end of the discovery period, the defendant will hire expert witnesses, such as doctors, who will examine you in order to discredit your case. Although these physical examinations may be called "independent medical examinations" (IMEs), they are hardly independent. The doctors chosen by the insurance companies are usually hired guns who should not be trusted for any advice concerning your injuries and medical conditions. The doctor will issue a written report discussing his or her findings. All IMEs and expert reports must be served on opposing counsel within twenty days from the discovery end date.

After discovery closes, the court will assign an "arbitration" date. This is an informal hearing at the courthouse before a private lawyer who has been selected by the court to be an arbitrator. The arbitration is nonbinding and either party is free to appeal the results. The arbitrator will meet with the lawyers before the arbitration to narrow the issues. The arbitrator will then bring in the litigants to hear their versions of the events by their sworn "testimony."

At the end of the arbitration, the arbitrator will consider the testimony, apply the law, and give his or her opinion as to the value of the case. That opinion is known as an arbitrator's award. If either party is dissatisfied with the arbitrator's award, that party can file an appeal within thirty days of the arbitration award and set it aside by paying the required filing fee and filing a document requesting a "trial de novo." The case will then be listed for trial.

Usually the court will try to bring the parties together toward resolution by scheduling a settlement conference before a judge. These conferences are often successful. However, if a case does not settle, the case will proceed toward trial.

Court orders can be issued if, during this litigation process, one of the parties chooses to ignore the demands and requests from the other party. In order to get a court order, the aggrieved party must file a "motion" for specific relief.

Once a case is assigned out for trial, the parties will have an opportunity to select a fair jury. The process of interviewing potential jurors is known as "jury voir dire." Both parties will make opening statements and call their witnesses, who will be examined and cross-examined by counsel. Since the plaintiff has the burden of proof, it is the plaintiff's obligation to put on an affirmative case first. Each defendant will then call witnesses, usually consisting of the defendant and medical expert witnesses. The parties will then have an opportunity to sum up or argue their positions in their "closing arguments" or "summations." The judge will then instruct the jury in what is known as a "jury charge" as to the law to be applied, which will be followed by the jury's deliberations and the jury's verdict.

After a verdict, the parties will prepare judgments that the court will sign in order to enter judgment. From that date, the appeal clock will start to run.

The above is a simplified version of the events. All lawyers and pro se parties are obligated to follow the New Jersey Court Rules, which is a published book containing over 2,600 pages of rules and commentary. Lawyers and pro se parties are expected to know and follow these rules. During September of each year, new court rules are published. For that reason, one should not rely solely upon the court procedures discussed in this book without researching their current status.

If your case is brought in federal court, please note that a totally different set of court rules will apply that may differ sharply from New Jersey's court rules.

SUMMARY

RULE: ALTHOUGH THERE IS NO LEGAL REQUIREMENT THAT ONE MUST BE A LAWYER TO USE THE COURT SYSTEM, A LITIGANT SHOULD NOT REPRESENT HIM OR HERSELF, AND SHOULD INSTEAD HIRE A QUALIFIED AND EXPERIENCED PERSONAL INJURY LAWYER.

CHAPTER TWENTY-FOUR

OTHER TYPES OF PERSONAL INJURY CLAIMS

Although automobile accidents are by far the most common type of personal injury claim, there are several other types of personal injury claims. The following represents a brief overview of a few other types of personal injury claims.

A. Trucking, Bus, Motorcycle, Train, Moped, Bicycle, Aircraft and Boat Accident Claims.

Accidents, other than automobile accidents are subject to the rules of ordinary negligence. No-fault insurance and its restrictive threshold only apply to automobile accidents. Each mode of transportation requires an understanding of safety issues associated with using that particular form of transportation. For example, jurors may be prejudiced against motorcycle operators, and because of that prejudice will wrongfully impose upon the motorcycle operator a higher standard of care. Experienced trial lawyers are sensitive to those issues.

A common type of transportation accident involves passenger buses. These accidents may involve public transportation or charter buses. Injuries may result from a collision, a roll over, or negligently discharging a passenger at an unsafe stop. Occasionally, an injury will occur due to the bus operator's error. An example of a driver's error would be an unnecessary short stop or prematurely closing a door on a passenger.

The law imposes upon certain types of common carriers, such as buses and rail services, a higher standard of care to guard against foreseeable harm. It is not uncommon to hire a skilled accident reconstructionist as an expert witness to determine and prove the true cause of an accident.

Accidents which occur on public transportation may be subject to the New Jersey Torts Claims Act including its required ninety day written notice provision; as well as a monetary and injury threshold. Accidents involving a New Jersey Port Authority bus or train are subject to a one year statute of limitations.

Transportation related accidents can also be caused by a mechanical defect. In order to prove a mechanical defect, a skilled trial lawyer would retain the services of a forensic mechanic. Even if a vehicle did not malfunction, there may still be a products liability case if the vehicle contained a design defect. In cases involving a catastrophic injury, such as, a collision causing a fuel tank explosion, a seat back to break, or a vehicle roll-over at a low speed, a skilled lawyer should consider investigating the possibility that an unsafe design caused or contributed to the accident. These cases are extremely complex and vigorously defended by the vehicle's manufacturer. They are also very expensive to pursue since they require lawyers to retain the services of highly skilled automotive design engineers.

The same holds true for aviation accidents which may be complicated by federal laws and international treaties. Although extremely rare, aviation collisions are often caused by pilot error or a mechanical or design defect. Small aircraft are not required to carry a flight data recorder, or a "black box." The lack of a flight data recorder often makes it difficult to determine the exact cause of a crash.

Although our waterways are quite safe, a large number of people suffer injuries on cruise ships, recreational boats, and ferry lines. These accidents are usually caused by human error. Accidents on large vessels, such as a cruise ship can occur due to improper maintenance, similar to accidents occurring in a store or mall. People may be caused to slip on water or grease causing a serious injury.

During the last few decades more people own small boats for recreation purposes. These vessels now include personal watercrafts, which include jet skis, that are basically motorcycles designed to operate on water. Recreational boating accidents usually involve a collision between two smaller vessels. Youthful and inexperienced drivers often cause injuries by taking unnecessary risks. As with many other recreational activities, people often mix alcohol with fun. Unfortunately, the combination of the two is often lethal. The good news is that more states now require operators of boats to take an approved boat safety course and pass a written examination.

Other non-automobile accidents can involve bicycles and mopeds. Usually these accidents involve an automobile. These cases are usually complicated by a police report blaming the bicycle, or moped operator. More often these accidents are caused by a distracted driver who was not alert to others sharing the road.

B. Fall Down and Premises Liability Claims.

These common claims involve injuries resulting from a slip, trip, or fall on another person's property or premises. These injuries could occur on a stairway, sidewalk, driveway, or any other negligently maintained walking surface. Quite often, people slip inside a store due to a liquid substance on the floor. People may be injured outside a store in a pothole or by slipping on ice or snow.

The law requires a homeowner or storekeeper to keep their property in a reasonably safe condition. Usually there are building and safety codes that property owners must follow.

Unfortunately, for those injured because of a slip, trip, or fall accident, the injuries can be quite serious. Typical injuries include broken bones, damage to tendons and ligaments, concussions, lacerations and abrasions, and injuries to the neck and back, such as herniated or ruptured discs.

In order to prove a premises liability case, it is important to hire an expert witness to examine the premises to determine the cause of the accident and the potential code violations. Injuries that occur during the evening may be the result of inadequate lighting.

There are unique and important safety requirements applicable to stairways, riser heights, handrails and stair surface materials that could be relevant in proving your case.

People injured because of a fall may have an initial inclination to feel embarrassment. For this reason, it is common for them not to promptly report an incident. If the dangerous conditions continue to exist, send someone over, as soon as possible, to take photographs. If you did not report the incident, contact the owner of the property or the storekeeper as soon as possible to report the incident.

Again, in order to properly safeguard your legal rights, you should consult with and hire a competent and qualified personal injury lawyer.

C. Workers' Compensation Claims.

If you were injured on the job, you are entitled to compensation for your losses through the New Jersey workers' compensation system. You are entitled to your full benefits and award even if your own mistakes or negligence caused your injuries.

Under New Jersey's workers' compensation laws you are entitled to receive temporary medical care, temporary disability benefits, and an award for permanent injuries through your employer's workers' compensation insurance policy.

Years ago, injured workers had few if any rights to compensation for their injuries. They were often fired and left with huge medical bills and no income. As a result, laws were passed to protect workers from these losses. The tradeoff is that a worker cannot sue the employer directly for damages unless the employer committed gross negligence or committed an act that would likely cause injury. Another tradeoff is that you generally do not have the option of selecting your own physician. You will be obligated to see only those doctors selected by your employer.

Again, these cases can be quite tricky. Often, property and cars are titled in the name of someone other than your employer. Under those circumstances, it may be possible to proceed with a "third-party lawsuit" against that person or entity. A third-party claim is a claim against another person or entity that alleges negligence on their part causing a worker to suffer an injury. That negligence may have been caused by an independent contractor's negligence, a land-lord's negligence, or by a defectively designed product or machine. If you were injured on the job, you should take the necessary steps to immediately contact a qualified workers' compensation lawyer who concentrates most of his or her time representing injured workers specifically before the judges of the Workers' Compensation Court. He or she may also be in a position to determine if there exists a viable third-party claim, and provide you with the necessary guidance and legal advice you will certainly require.

D. Medical Malpractice Claims

Unfortunately, from time to time, doctors and hospital staff make mistakes. Even more unfortunate is that the consequences of those mistakes can be quite severe or fatal. People who suffer injuries because of medical malpractice have a right to bring a claim for their harms and losses. However, be assured that the complexities and standards of proof required to win a medical malpractice case can constitute a major obstacle.

Medical malpractice cases can arise out of a misdiagnosis, a mix-up in tests, a complication during surgery, improper administration of medications, or a failure to provide adequate informed consent prior to a medical procedure or operation.

It's not enough to win a medical malpractice case by just proving that a doctor was negligent. The standard of proof is that you must show that the doctor, nurse, or medical technician failed to act in a reasonable manner and acted contrary to the standards and practices of other medical providers in that same community. In technical terms, "Negligence is conduct which deviates from a standard of care required by law for the protection of persons from harm."[21]

Medical negligence cases are extremely complex and vigorously defended by doctors and their insurance companies. To bring a medical malpractice case, the plaintiff must first obtain, within sixty days of the filing of the complaint, an "affidavit of merit" from a similar physician setting forth the alleged deviation from those generally acceptable medical practices. Both sides will try to hire the best and most credible expert witnesses, which could cost tens and possibly hundreds of thousands of dollars.

Only a lawyer or law firm with sufficient experience and skill in representing medical malpractice victims should venture into this area.

One final note about medical negligence cases is that under certain circumstances, the usual statute of limitations of two years can be extended to start from the date you first learned of the alleged misconduct on the part of the hospital or physician. This is called the "discovery rule."

E. Products Liability Claims.

When someone is injured during the course of operating a machine or using a product, he or she may have a viable products liability claim.

---

21   N.J. Model Jury Charge (Civil) Medical Negligence §5.50A
"Duty and Negligence" (March 2002)

Quite often, lawyers see these types of cases when people are injured because of improperly designed safety mechanisms in cars or machines. Failures of seatbelts or air bags, tire blowouts, roof crushes, sudden acceleration, or vehicular explosions may have been avoided if the manufacturer merely designed or built the product correctly. If a product is proven to be inherently unsafe then the manufacturer of the product is "strictly liable" for all injuries caused by the product.

Other types of products liability cases include cases against drug manufacturers. Years ago, claims were proven that a popular diet drug known as Fen-Phen was unsafe and dangerous. Another unsafe medication case followed when the FDA recalled Vioxx. Since there are hundreds and even thousands of claimants, these cases are also referred to as "mass tort cases."

Other products liability cases involve defectively designed machines used by workers during the course of their employment. Although a worker is entitled to bring a workers' compensation claim, he or she may also be entitled to bring a separate claim against the manufacturer of the machine in a "third-party suit."

Other products liability cases may deal with the wholesomeness of food products. A food poisoning case is really a product liability claim. Although most food poisoning cases involve temporary discomfort, an Ebola food poisoning case can have serious long-term medical consequences.

Products liability cases, like medical negligence cases, are extremely complex and should be handled only by an experienced and qualified lawyer.

F. Animal Attacks and Dog Bite Claims.

In New Jersey, if an animal bite penetrates the skin, the owner of a dog is strictly liable for all injuries resulting from the animal attack. Being strictly liable means that the conduct of the person who was bitten is not of any significant relevance. The fact that he or she was attacked is sufficient to win the case. There may be other defenses, such as trespass; however, once it is determined that the legal doctrine of "strict liability" applies, the case becomes a damages only case.

Dog bite cases present unique challenges because most jurors at some point in their lives were part of a family that owned a dog. These potential jurors may have a bias in favor of the dog owner since they themselves have loved and enjoyed close relationships with their dogs.

G. Liquor and Over Serving Liability Claims.

Owners and operators of a business establishment, such as a tavern or club that serves alcohol, have an obligation to refuse to serve drinks to someone who appears to be visibly intoxicated. If they serve that person and that person goes out and injures another, including him or herself, there may be a claim made against the server of the alcohol. These cases are commonly known as "Dram Shop cases."

The same rules apply with some minor changes to social hosts. Homeowners and others can be held responsible for the damages, injuries, or death of another if they over serve alcohol to guests or if a minor consumes alcohol on their premises.

Under certain circumstances, "punitive damages" may be awarded. These cases are also extremely complex and may call for expert opinions by medical doctors and toxicologists. Again, only a skilled and experienced personal injury lawyer should venture into this area of the law.

H. Construction and Worksite Injury Claims.

One of the most dangerous places to work is at an active construction site. Construction workers often work outdoors during all seasons. They work on construction sites with numerous other building trades. Their work often takes place within unprotected areas, without stairs or external walls. To perform their jobs and build their structures they may be required to use temporary scaffolds and ladders. As a result, construction workers are at an exceptional risk of suffering a serious and catastrophic injury from a coworker, a fall, or a defective product. Certain states, such as New York, have labor laws that provide benefits to construction workers regardless of fault.[22]

For the most part, it is the obligation of the general contractor to make certain that the premises are safe for workers and subcontractors. Strict state and federal standards, including "OSHA" (Occupational Safety and Health Administration) laws, protect the safety of workers. Sometimes, general contractors will ignore these laws and may cut corners in order to save time or money.

Unfortunately, all too often the person who pays the price of those savings is the worker who was injured because of the misconduct of the general contractor or possibly the employee's direct employer.

In order to prove a construction site injury case, it is often necessary to retain the services of an OSHA expert who will examine the government's records, review all of the discovery within the case, and read through all testimony of the parties and witnesses to formulate an opinion as to the cause and responsibility for the accident.

Again, construction site cases can be quite tricky and should be handled only by an experienced and qualified personal injury lawyer.

I. Supermarket, Shopping Mall, and Store Accident Claims.

Many people shop out of necessity in order to purchase the goods and merchandise needed for their families, while others visit malls for pleasure, exercise, or just to socialize. People who visit

---

22   New York Labor Laws 240(1) and 241(6) are the most common construction accident statutes employed in such lawsuits.

a business establishment or mall have the right to expect that the store or mall will be maintained and operated in a clean, safe, and responsible manner.

A storekeeper in New Jersey must treat shoppers as invitees. This means that the storekeeper has a reasonable duty to discover unsafe conditions and to repair them before a customer becomes injured. This duty extends to the interior of the store as well as the parking facilities. Common injuries that occur within a store include injuries caused by a liquid on the floor that a customer may slip on, improperly stacked merchandise that may fall onto a customer, low stacks that customers trip over, and injuries caused by the mechanical doors.

A common defense by a storekeeper is that the customer contributed to the accident by not making the appropriate observations within the store. This is not a fair defense because storekeepers study shoppers' habits and purposely design displays to catch the attention of their patrons. As a result of these visual merchandise displays, a customer normally concentrates his or her attention on the shelves and not the floor.

Outside injuries can occur due to improperly removed ice or snow, stray shopping carts knocking down and injuring customers, or assaults taking place in an improperly lit common parking lot area in which criminal activity is foreseeable.

The good news is that because of years of litigation against storekeepers the number of accident-related claims has dramatically dropped. Stores are cleaner and better lit. Interior spills are promptly cleaned up and outside snow and ice are thoroughly and promptly removed. Children are no longer being cut by sharp display edges, and interior floors are now polished with slip-retardant wax.

Through the years, injuries in supermarkets have decreased, proving that many accidents are clearly avoidable. We can thank our civil justice system for being the vehicle for this social improvement.

Owners of well managed businesses have taken responsibility for the safety of their stores. Safer stores cause fewer customers, including the elderly, to fall and suffer life changing injuries. A well managed store usually insures that customers can enjoy a safe and clean shopping experience without fear of being injured.

J. Wrongful Death Claims.

The most common types of wrongful death claims involve medical malpractice, often resulting from one of the following: a doctor's improper diagnosis, birth accidents, medication side effects, nursing home negligence, or just about any type of injury that became severe enough to cause a person to lose his or her life.

From a personal injury lawyer's point of view, there is no greater tragedy than the unnecessary loss of a life due to the negligence of another person. These cases are highly emotional for the surviving family members, the defendant who caused the death, as well as the lawyers involved. Many times, the true facts surrounding a death are concealed, or worse, conveniently changed within official records to protect or immunize a defendant. Making matters even more difficult is the fact that wrongful death victims will often die from their injuries before they can explain how their accidents happened. As a result, lawyers and their investigators are often required to piece together the facts to determine exactly how an accident happened.

If an accident victim died without a will, issues as simple as deciding which family member will be appointed to serve as the "Administrator ad Prosequendum," or the legal representative of the estate, can be very difficult, especially if the surviving family members include children from a prior marriage, separated spouses, or children born to unmarried parents. The administrator of the estate ultimately makes the important decisions such as which lawyer to hire, and later, the final decision authorizing a settlement.

Certain occupations, by the nature of the work itself, are extremely dangerous. Construction site accidents, such as burns or a fall from a scaffold are challenging since the applicable liability laws of each state will determine different outcomes. Workers' compensation laws in one state may prevent a worker from suing his or her employer for damages in that state; however, had the accident happened in a different state, the worker may have been able to sue the employer or co-workers for damages.

The amount to which family members are entitled to claim due to the loss of a loved one also differs from state to state. In New Jersey, two distinct claims can be brought as a result of an accidental death. These claims are known as the "wrongful death" claim and the "survival" claim.

The wrongful death claim is for the future financial losses suffered by the family of the decedent, while the survival claim is for his or her pre-death pain and any financial losses suffered by the decedent.

Wrongful death damages in New Jersey consist of the future financial losses to a surviving spouse and any financially dependent children of the deceased. In New Jersey, surviving family members are not allowed to make a claim for their emotional losses. However, they can make a claim for quantifiable future dollar losses. Often they must prove these losses by hiring an economist who will serve as an expert witness to arrive at a dollar amount valuing the loss.

As an expert witness, the economist will put an hourly value on the future lost services of the decedent for any companionship services to a spouse, homemaking services, advice and counsel, plus the loss of future earnings that would have been used to support a surviving spouse or dependent children.

Again, there is no right to compensation for the emotional pain experienced by a decedent's family unless they happen to have been eyewitnesses to the accident.

For an understanding about just how complicated the valuation of a case can be for a jury, one must examine the actual jury instruction given to a jury by the trial judge before the jury begins their final deliberations. Here is what a judge instructs a jury *not* to consider in any wrongful death case:

8.43 Wrongful Death (Approved 3/2010)
What Is Not Recoverable

A. In this category of damages, you are not to consider any physical injuries or suffering that the decedent may have sustained, such as pain and suffering or disability.

B. You are also not to consider any emotional distress, anguish, or grief the survivors may have suffered as a result of the decedent's death, or any loss of emotional satisfaction the survivors may have derived from the society and companionship of the decedent. These matters, although very real and distressing, cannot be considered in determining the extent of the financial loss suffered by the survivors.[23]

Another part to a death claim is known as the survival action. This part of a claim is brought by the administrator of the estate for the pain and suffering experienced by the decedent prior to his or her death. This claim is not only for the decedent's pre-death pain and suffering, but also for the economic losses suffered by the deceased up until the time of his or her death.

Before a jury values a survival action, they will hear the judge specifically instruct them that they must apply the following law:

---

23   Model Jury Charge (Civil) 8:43 (A) "Wrongful Death" (March 2010) for full text of Section 8:43 (A) see Appendix G.

8.42 SURVIVAL ACTION (Approved 2/96)

> In a survival action, the administrator as plaintiff is seeking damages for the decedent's hospital and medical expenses, loss of earnings as well as any disability and impairment, loss of enjoyment, and pain and suffering which the decedent sustained between this accident and his/her death. Under the law, he/she is entitled to recover the damages which the decedent sustained during this period of time.[24]

The current law in New Jersey is particularly unfair and cruel because if a person died instantly from an accident, the formula for evaluating damages allows only for the actual future economic losses suffered by the dependent surviving spouse and children. So in effect, under the current New Jersey law, there could be little or no provable economic loss if the decedent was a young child, a disabled adult, a retired senior citizen, a young unmarried adult, or a homemaker. Making matters worse, under the current New Jersey law, the economic loss is further compromised if the decedent had no dependents such as a spouse or minor children.

Under certain circumstances, such as a death caused by a drunk or intoxicated driver, a jury may be asked to consider and award punitive damages. These damages are specifically designed to punish and set an example to others of the consequence of the reckless disregard of the rights of another.

For these reasons, wrongful death and survival cases can be extremely complicated and should not be handled by anyone other than an experienced New Jersey personal injury lawyer.

Despite the obstacles of the current New Jersey wrongful death laws, a skilled lawyer can study a person's life and with the help of

---

24   Model Jury Charge(Civil) 8.42 "Survival Action" (February 1996)

an appropriate economist determine the true financial loss of not only future earnings, but the loss to the family of the society, companionship, and services of a loved one.

Although no amount of money can ever fully compensate a family for the loss of a parent or child, the process does provide the family with a sense of justice, which eventually helps bring closure to the situation.

A lawyer can feel satisfied if he or she helped a grieving family find the answers they so desire, held the wrongdoer financially accountable, and helped the family reach the closure they need so that they can honor the memory of their loved one, yet continue with their own lives.

SUMMARY

RULE: THERE ARE MANY VARIETIES OF PERSONAL INJURY CASES AND EACH IS SUBJECT TO ITS OWN UNIQUE SET OF LAWS.

RULE: SINCE PERSONAL INJURY LAW IN NEW JERSEY IS EXTREMELY COMPLICATED AND EVER CHANGING, ANYONE WHO HAS SUFFERED AN INJURY BECAUSE OF ANOTHER'S NEGLIGENCE SHOULD, AS SOON AS POSSIBLE, CONTACT A PERSONAL INJURY LAWYER FOR A FREE CONSULTATION TO LEARN ABOUT HIS OR HER RIGHTS AND TO PROTECT HIS OR HER INTERESTS.

Garry R. Salomon

Some Final Thoughts...

So there you have it. I hope that after you read this book you have a better understanding of tort law and the New Jersey legal system. The successful conclusion of a personal injury case requires active participation by both an attorney and an informed client. The more a client knows about the law and the more a client understands how the system works, the more a client can participate in the case.

My experience has taught me that all lawyers should strive to educate their clients, starting with the very first interview. Lawyers could avoid most fatal mistakes made in personal injury cases by merely taking time to talk to their clients to raise and evaluate any potential harmful issues.

Although our tort system is a topic of heated controversy, we all have directly benefited from it. Cars are safer, doctors are more cautious, machines have safety guards, product designs are safer, property owners maintain their property better, roads are repaved sooner, and people have learned to respect the safety of others.

Police departments fight crime, not negligence. City officials may issue tickets for dangerous code violations, but neither governmental agency worries about the accident victim. That measure of justice is left to the civil justice system. For each case a trial lawyer accepts, he or she is fighting not only for justice on behalf of a client, but for the general safety of the public at large.

Our legal system is not perfect and there are those who seek change through "tort reform" aimed at taking away the consumer's right to sue for damages. Yet, others see the system as a way to level the playing field between a multinational corporation and an individual. Like it or not, for most people who suffered a wrong, the system worked when they received a fair settlement. If you ask a judge, "What's the definition of a fair settlement?" he or she would likely reply: "A settlement is fair if a defendant believes that he or she paid too much and at the same time the plaintiff believes that he or she received too little."

On the other hand, many believe that a fair settlement is when a client believes that he or she was treated fairly and got the justice he or she deserved. Hopefully, you will receive the same. I also hope that reading this book has given you some insight into the legal process so that your case will neither be lost nor diminished due to lack of knowledge.

Don't be afraid to talk to your lawyer. There is no such thing as a stupid question. I urge you to discuss all issues with your lawyer and get the just compensation you deserve.

GLOSSARY OF USEFUL TERMS

AAJ – The American Association for Justice (formerly known as the Association of Trial Lawyers of America) is a national organization of lawyers who represent accident victims.

Accident – An occurrence caused by someone's negligence.

Affidavit – A sworn written statement signed under the penalty of perjury, in the presence of a notary public.

Adjuster –A representative of an insurance company whose job it is to settle a claim made under an insurance policy.

Administrator – An individual appointed by the Surrogate Court to wind up the affairs of a deceased person who died without a will.

Administrator ad Prosequendum – An individual appointed by the Surrogate Court to bring a wrongful death lawsuit on behalf of a person who died as the result of someone else's negligence.

Appeal – A request that a higher court review the findings of a lower court.

Arbitration – An informal proceeding used to save time and money in an attempt to resolve disputes in place of a trial before a judge or jury.

At Fault Driver – The negligent driver who caused an accident.

Attorney – An individual who has completed four years of undergraduate studies and three additional years of an ABA-approved law school, passed the bar exam, and was found to be fit to practice law by the supreme court of a particular state.

Bodily Injury Liability – Insurance coverage that pays claims to a person for injuries caused by another driver's negligence.

Carrier – An insurance company.

Certification of Permanency – A sworn statement signed by a physician to be filed with the court stating that the plaintiff suffered an injury that is permanent, and that the body part affected will no longer heal to function normally.

Certified Civil Trial Attorney – A New Jersey attorney who has practiced law for over five years, tried over ten cases, taken and passed a written examination and continuing legal education requirements, and has been certified by the New Jersey Supreme Court as a Civil Trial Attorney after undergoing a thorough background investigation, including references from judges and adversaries.

Civil Action – A lawsuit brought for money damages.

Claim – The assertion of a right; a demand for payment in accordance with an insurance policy or a demand for something as rightful or due to another.

Collision Coverage – Under this type of automobile coverage, your own insurance company will pay for any property damage to your car subject to a deductible. Collision coverage is generally subject to a deductible and may be expensive to purchase.

Comparative Negligence – Any negligent act or conduct on the part of the person making a claim that may have contributed to the cause of the accident.

Complaint – The first pleading filed with the clerk of the court by a plaintiff setting forth his or her allegations against a specific person or entity including theories of negligence.

Comprehensive Coverage – covers theft, fire, vandalism, weather damage, riots, missiles, and other similar circumstances which may cause damage to a vehicle. Comprehensive auto insurance does not usually cover acts of God, theft or vandalism by family members or employees, contents of the vehicle, tires, or damage due to improper maintenance.

Contingent Fee – A fee charged for a lawyer's services only if the lawsuit is successful or is favorably settled out of court.

Damages – The physical and financial losses suffered by a plaintiff.

Decedent – A dead or deceased person.

Defendant – The person who is being sued in a lawsuit.

Defense Counsel – The attorneys who are hired to represent a defendant.

Deposition – An out-of-court sworn oral statement of a party or a witness in connection with a lawsuit, which a court reporter is transcribing.

Discovery – A period of time after the filing of a lawsuit during which the parties can investigate facts through interrogatories, depositions, document requests, and subpoenas.

Entire Controversy Doctrine – The legal principle that requires a plaintiff or defendant to bring all claims or defenses as part of any first proceeding. The effect of not bringing all claims at once is to bar any subsequent trials, hearings, or proceedings for any losses or injuries not alleged in the initial proceeding.

ERISA – Benefits paid to an employee as part of a qualified employer-sponsored benefit program under the Employee Retirement Income Security Act of 1974.

Essential Services Coverage – A type of benefit that is part of New Jersey's personal injury protection (PIP), reimbursing the cost of needed household and domestic help.

Executor – A person named in a will to wind up the affairs of a deceased person and to carry out the directives of the deceased's last will and testament.

Expert Witness – An individual hired in connection with a lawsuit to provide factual and opinion testimony in connection with a topic outside of the normal knowledge of a juror.

Federal Court – Courts created by an act of Congress to prosecute federal crimes and resolve civil disputes against the federal government, constitutional claims, and disputes between citizens of different states.

Filing – The physical act of delivering to the clerk of a court a pleading or document for the court's consideration.

Filing Fee – The sum of money required to be paid to the clerk of the court before a document can be accepted by the clerk and deemed to be filed.

First-Party Claim – A claim that is brought against one's own insurance carrier or against a carrier obligated by law or contract to pay a claim, such as a workers' compensation or PIP insurance carrier.

Friendly – A special hearing conducted by a judge to determine the fairness of a settlement made for the benefit of a minor.

GAP Insurance – A type of property damage insurance coverage that in the event of a total loss of a vehicle will pay the difference between the vehicle's actual cash value and the current outstanding balance on any loan or lease.

IME – ("independent medical examination") Although called independent, such examinations should be properly called a DME or defense medical examination, which is a medical examination at the request of the defense that is usually biased in favor of the defense.

Income Continuation Benefits – A New Jersey no-fault insurance benefit available to accident victims regardless of fault to partially compensate for lost wages resulting from an accident.

Infant – A minor; a child under the age of eighteen.

Infant Compromise – A settlement of a personal injury lawsuit for the benefit of a child.

Insurance – A contract in which an individual or entity pays money in advance to another to receive financial protection or reimbursement for unforeseen losses or claims.

Interrogatories – Written questions that are part of the discovery process, to be answered under oath and in writing as required under the New Jersey Rules of Court.

Jury Charge – The instructions given by the judge to a jury prior to deliberations as to what laws to apply during the jury's deliberations.

Judgment – A decision or order signed by a judge that determines the rights and obligations of the litigants. A jury verdict is enforceable and collectible only after a judge "enters judgment."

Lawsuit Threshold – Also known as the "verbal threshold" or "limitation on lawsuit threshold," it is a restriction on the ability to bring a lawsuit for automobile accident-related injuries unless such injuries fall within one of six listed exceptions or are permanent injuries to body parts that will not heal to function normally again, as certified to by a physician.

Lien – An outstanding sum of money that attaches to a case and must be paid out of the final settlement proceeds.

Limitation on Lawsuit Threshold – See definition of lawsuit threshold above.

Loss – The payment of any claim by an insurance company.

Motion – A pleading filed with the court seeking a specified ruling or court order most commonly used to compel opposing counsel to provide discovery.

MRI – Magnetic Resonance Imaging; a type of imaging machine using magnetic force to produce internal soft tissue images which are interpreted by a radiologist.

NADA – National Automobile Dealers Association is a service used by insurance companies to value used automobiles.

Narrative Report – A report prepared by a treating or non-treating doctor who has been hired as an expert witness for a fee, which discusses a person's injuries, the cause of such injuries, as well as the permanency of those injuries.

Negligence – The failure to exercise the standard of care that a reasonably prudent person would have exercised.

NJAJ – The New Jersey Association for Justice (formerly the Association of Trial Lawyers of America-New Jersey).

No-Fault Insurance – A type of automobile insurance that is compulsory in New Jersey, where policyholders are reimbursed for their medical bills, lost wages, essential services, and death benefits by the policyholder's own insurance company without proof of fault. In exchange, a policyholder or resident family members may not be permitted to seek recovery through the civil justice system for those damages and may be limited in recovering for their pain and suffering caused by others.

Objective Tests – Objective medical tests such as MRI, X-ray, or CT scans are tests that are not based on the person's voluntary responses, such as pain. Objective medical tests cannot be faked or exaggerated.

OSHA – The Occupational Safety and Health Administration is a federal agency of the United States that regulates workplace safety and health.

Parties – The litigants involved in a lawsuit.

Personal Injury Protection – Known as "PIP" benefits, are insurance benefits payable as part of New Jersey's no-fault automobile insurance consisting of medical bill payment, income continuation benefits, funeral benefits, and essential services payable regardless of fault.

PIP – See personal injury protection above.

PIP SUIT – A legal proceeding usually in the form of arbitration against an automobile insurance carrier to force them to pay justified no-fault insurance benefits.

Pleading – A formal written statement filed with the court by a party in a civil action, such as a complaint or answer.

PLIGA – The Property Liability Insurance Guarantee Association is a New Jersey State entity that pays claims involving uninsured drivers, insolvent insurance companies, and the medical bills of uninsured pedestrians struck by automobiles.

Premises Liability – An accident that occurred due to the negligence of a landowner or storekeeper.

Preponderance of Evidence – The standard of proof required in a civil trial that proves a fact or event "more likely than not."

Pro Se – An individual representing him or herself before a court without a lawyer.

Punitive Damages – Damages awarded in addition to actual damages when a defendant acted with malice, recklessness, or gross indifference for life and limb. Punitive damages are meant to punish and set an example to deter others from such harmful conduct.

Property Damage Liability – Insurance coverage that pays for physical damage to another person's property or motor vehicle that was caused by the policyholder's negligence.

Retainer Agreement – A written agreement that hires the services of an attorney and sets forth how the attorney will be paid.

Release – A written document that, when signed, discharges a person or entity from any further legal responsibility or liability.

Reserve – The amount of money an insurance company sets aside in anticipation of paying a claim.

Serve – To make legal delivery of a document, pleading, notice, summons, complaint, or subpoena upon another person or entity in the fashion and format as prescribed by the rules of court.

Settlement – An agreement between the parties to end a legal dispute or lawsuit.

Settlement Conference – A conference held before a judge to narrow the differences between the parties in hope of reaching a settlement.

Soft Tissue – Body parts other than bone, such as nerves, muscles, blood vessels, and the brain.

Statute of Limitations – A law that establishes a time limit for suing in a civil case.

Strict Liability – Liability that does not depend upon the actual negligence or intent of another but is based upon a breach of a duty to make something or some situation absolutely safe. Strict liability is commonly found in cases involving products liability, dog bites, and New York's labor law, which covers injuries arising from scaffold falls and construction site injuries.

Structured Settlement – A tax-free settlement that will be paid in future periodic payments.

Subpoena – A legal document that compels a person or corporation to appear at a designated time and place, for the purpose of giving testimony or producing documents.

Subrogation – A legal right acquired when an insurance carrier that paid a first-party claim is assigned by the injured party the right to pursue a lawsuit against the responsible party to recover the money they paid.

Summation – A lawyer's closing arguments at the conclusion of a trial.

Summons – A notice requiring a person to appear in court or answer a lawsuit.

Surrogate – A special court established in New Jersey whose jurisdiction includes the probate of wills, appointment of estate administrators, supervision of the appointment of guardians, and administration of adoptions. In the context of personal injury claims, the surrogate will hold a minor's settlement funds in an interest-bearing account until the minor reaches the age of eighteen.

Survival Action or Survivorship Claim – An action brought by a deceased person's estate for injuries or damages suffered by them between the time of the accident and the person's death.

Third-Party Lawsuit – A claim brought against an insurance carrier other than your own. In the context of a workers' compensation claim, it is a claim brought against anyone other than the injured person's employer or the employer's workers' compensation carrier.

Threshold – A minimum standard that must be met before a claim or defense can proceed.

Torts – A civil wrong arising out of a breach of a duty or act of negligence for which an injured party is entitled to an award of damages.

Tort Claims Act – A law that permits a lawsuit against a state, county, municipality, political subdivision, or governmental agency that would ordinarily be immune from a claim for damages.

Tort Claims Notice – The required written notice on a special form that must be filed within ninety days of an act of negligence of or by an employee of the State of New Jersey, a political subdivision, or a governmental agency that caused an injury or harm to another.

Tort Reform – A movement to reduce the amount of tort litigation by passing anti-consumer laws to restrict or take away the right of individuals to access the courts for damages awards.

Trial de Novo – A new trial ordered on the entire case usually resulting from an appeal of an unfavorable arbitration award.

Verbal Threshold – Also known as the "lawsuit threshold" or "limitation on lawsuit threshold," the verbal threshold is a restriction on the ability to bring a lawsuit for automobile accident-related injuries unless such injuries fall within one of six listed exceptions or are permanent injuries to body parts that will not heal to function normally again, as certified by a physician.

Verdict – The final findings of a jury regarding questions of fact and damages after applying the law as read to them by the judge.

Under Insured Motorist Coverage (UIM) – Insurance coverage that pays for losses and injuries caused by a negligent driver who lacks sufficient insurance coverage to cover the damages.

Uninsured Motorist Coverage (UM) – Insurance coverage that pays for losses and injuries caused by a negligent driver who was uninsured at the time of an accident.

Venue – The county having jurisdiction or location of a legal forum where a trial on a particular matter will occur.

Voir Dire – The pretrial interview conducted by the court of potential jurors to evaluate their fairness, fitness, and impartiality prior to being selected as jurors.

Workers' Compensation – A system for providing benefits to workers who are injured on the job, regardless of fault.

Wrongful Death Claim – A lawsuit on behalf of a deceased person's survivors for the future economic losses they will suffer, that is brought against the negligent party who caused the death.

Zero Threshold – Having selected no threshold or not being legally subject to a threshold that would act as a legal bar or obstruction to bringing a claim or lawsuit. In the context of an automobile claim, a zero threshold automatically satisfies the verbal or lawsuit threshold.

APPENDICES

APPENDIX A

NJ MUNICIPALITY POLICE ACCIDENT REPORT GRID

To view online visit www.njlegalquestions.com

APPENDIX B

NJ STATE POLICE ACCIDENT REPORT CODE GRID

To view online visit www.njlegalquestions.com

NJ STATE POLICE ACCIDENT REPORT CODE GRID

Page 2 of 2

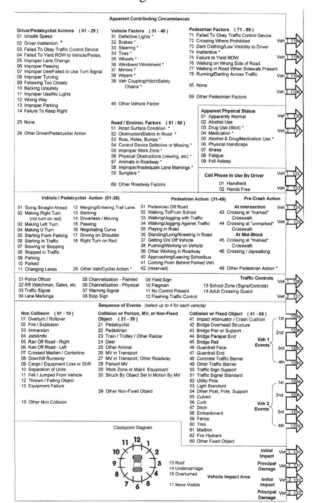

Apparent Contributing Circumstances

Driver/Pedalcyclist Actions (01 - 29)
01 Unsafe Speed
02 Driver Inattention *
03 Failed To Obey Traffic Control Device
04 Failed To Yield ROW to Vehicle/Pedes.
05 Improper Lane Change
06 Improper Passing
07 Improper Use/Failed to Use Turn Signal
08 Improper Turning
09 Following Too Closely
10 Backing Unsafely
11 Improper Use/No Lights
12 Wrong Way
13 Improper Parking
14 Failure To Keep Right

25 None

29 Other Driver/Pedalcyclist Action

Vehicle Factors (31 - 49)
31 Defective Lights *
32 Brakes *
33 Steering *
34 Tires *
35 Wheels *
36 Windows/ Windshield *
37 Mirrors *
38 Wipers *
39 Veh Coupling/Hitch/Safety Chains *

49 Other Vehicle Factor

Road / Environ. Factors (51 - 69)
51 Road Surface Condition *
52 Obstruction/Debris In Road *
53 Ruts, Holes, Bumps *
54 Control Device Defective or Missing *
55 Improper Work Zone *
56 Physical Obstructions (viewing, etc) *
57 Animals in Roadway *
58 Improper/Inadequate Lane Markings *
59 Sunglare *

69 Other Roadway Factors

Pedestrian Factors (71 - 89)
71 Failed To Obey Traffic Control Device
72 Crossing Where Prohibited
73 Dark Clothing/Low Visibility to Driver
74 Inattentive *
75 Failure to Yield ROW
76 Walking on Wrong Side of Road
77 Walking in Road When Sidewalk Present
78 Running/Darting Across Traffic

85 None

89 Other Pedestrian Factors

Apparent Physical Status
01 Apparently Normal
02 Alcohol Use
03 Drug Use (Illicit) *
04 Medication *
05 Alcohol & Drug/Medication Use *
06 Physical Handicaps
07 Illness
08 Fatigue
09 Fell Asleep

Cell Phone In Use By Driver
01 Handheld
02 Hands Free

Veh 1 119a
Veh 1 119b
Veh 2 119a
Veh 2 119b
Veh 1 120
Veh 2 121
Veh 1 122
Veh 2 123

Vehicle / Pedalcyclist Action (01-29)

01 Going Straight Ahead
02 Making Right Turn (not turn on red)
03 Making Left Turn
04 Making U Turn
05 Starting From Parking
06 Starting In Traffic
07 Slowing or Stopping
08 Stopped in Traffic
09 Parking
10 Parked
11 Changing Lanes
12 Merging/Entering Traf Lane
13 Backing
14 Driverless / Moving
15 Passing
16 Negotiating Curve
17 Driving on Shoulder
18 Right Turn on Red

29 Other Veh/Cyclist Action *

Pedestrian Action (31-49)

31 Pedestrian Off Road
32 Walking To/From School
33 Walking/Jogging with Traffic
34 Walking/Jogging Against Traffic
35 Playing in Road
36 Standing/Lying/Kneeling in Road
37 Getting On/ Off Vehicle
38 Pushing/Working on Vehicle
39 Other Working in Roadway
40 Approaching/Leaving Schoolbus
41 Coming From Behind Parked Veh.
42 (reserved)

Pre-Crash Action

43 Crossing at "marked" Crosswalk
44 Crossing at "unmarked" Crosswalk
At Mid-Block
45 Crossing at "marked" Crosswalk
46 Crossing / Jaywalking

49 Other Pedestrian Action *

Veh 1 124
Veh 2 125

Traffic Controls

01 Police Officer
02 RR Watchman, Gates, etc
03 Traffic Signal
04 Lane Markings
05 Channelization - Painted
06 Channelization - Physical
07 Warning Signal
08 Stop Sign
09 Yield Sign
10 Flagman
11 No Control Present
12 Flashing Traffic Control
13 School Zone (Signs/Controls)
14 Adult Crossing Guard

Veh 1 126
Veh 2 127

Sequence of Events (select up to 4 for each vehicle)

Non Collision (01 - 19)
01 Overturn / Rollover
02 Fire / Explosion
03 Immersion
04 Jackknife
05 Ran Off Road - Right
06 Ran Off Road - Left
07 Crossed Median / Centerline
08 Downhill Runaway
09 Cargo / Equipment Loss or Shift
10 Separation of Units
11 Fell / Jumped From Vehicle
12 Thrown / Falling Object
13 Equipment Failure

19 Other Non Collision

Collision w/ Person, MV, or Non-Fixed Object (21 - 39)
21 Pedalcyclist
22 Pedestrian
23 Train / Trolley / Other Railcar
24 Deer
25 Other Animal
26 MV in Transport
27 MV in Transport, Other Roadway
28 Parked MV
29 Work Zone or Maint. Equipment
30 Struck By Object Set In Motion By MV

39 Other Non-Fixed Object

Collision w/ Fixed Object (41 - 69)
41 Impact Attenuator / Crash Cushion
42 Bridge Overhead Structure
43 Bridge Pier or Support
44 Bridge Parapet End
45 Bridge Rail
46 Guardrail Face
47 Guardrail End
48 Concrete Traffic Barrier
49 Other Traffic Barrier
50 Traffic Sign Support
51 Traffic Signal Standard
52 Utility Pole
53 Light Standard
54 Other Post, Pole, Support
55 Culvert
56 Curb
57 Ditch
58 Embankment
59 Fence
60 Tree
61 Mailbox
62 Fire Hydrant
69 Other Fixed Object

Veh 1 Events 1st 128a
2nd 128b
3rd 128c
4th 128d

Veh 2 Events 1st 129a
2nd 129b
3rd 129c
4th 129d

Clockpoint Diagram

11 12 1
10 2
9 3
8 4
7 6 5

13 Roof
14 Undercarriage
15 Overturned
17 None Visible

Vehicle Impact Area

Initial Impact Veh 1 130
Principal Damage Veh 1 131
Initial Impact Veh 2 132
Principal Damage Veh 2 133

PRE-EXISTING CONDITIONS MODEL JURY CHARGES

8.1 IF DAMAGES CHARGES — GENERAL AGGRAVATION OF THE PREEXISTING DISABILITY (Approved 1/97)

In this case, evidence has been presented that plaintiff had an illness, / injury(ies) / condition before the accident/ incident — that is [describe the alleged preexisting injury]. I will refer to this condition as the preexisting injury. There are different rules for awarding damages depending on whether the preexisting injury was or was not causing plaintiff any harm or symptoms at the time of this accident.

Obviously, the defendants in this case are not responsible for any preexisting injury of [plaintiff]. As a result, you may not award any money in this case for damages attributable solely to any preexisting illness / injury(ies) / condition.

I will now explain what happens if the [plaintiff] was experiencing symptoms of the preexisting condition at the time of the accident. If the injuries sustained in this accident aggravated or made [plaintiff's] preexisting injury more severe, then the [plaintiff] may recover for any damages sustained due to an aggravation or worsening of a preexisting illness / injury(ies) / condition but only to the extent of that aggravation. Plaintiff has the burden of proving what portion of his/her condition is due to his / her preexisting injury. [Plaintiff] is entitled to damages only for that portion of his/her injuries attributable to the accident.

If you find that [plaintiff's] preexisting illness/injury(ies)/condition was not causing him/her any harm or symptoms at the time of the accident, but that the preexisting condition combined with injuries incurred in the accident to cause him/her damage, then [plaintiff] is entitled to recover for the full extent of the damages he/she sustained.

Jury Charge for Unknown Pre-Existing Conditions

[Use the following where a preexisting latent condition which caused no symptoms is involved].

I will now explain what happens if [plaintiff] had a predisposition or weakness which was causing no symptoms or problems before the accident but made him/her more susceptible to the kind of medical problems he/she claims in this case. If the injuries sustained in this accident combined with that predisposition to create the plaintiff's medical condition, then plaintiff is entitled to recover for all of the damage sustained due to that condition. You must not speculate that an individual without such predisposition or latent condition would have experienced less pain, suffering, disability and impairment.

NEW JERSEY
CONTINGENT FEE RULE

New Jersey Court Rule 1:21-7. Contingent Fees

(a) As used in this rule the term "contingent fee arrangement" means an agreement for legal services of an attorney or attorneys, including any associated or forwarding counsel, under which compensation, contingent in whole or in part upon the successful accomplishment or disposition of the subject matter of the agreement, is to be in an amount which either is fixed or is to be determined under a formula.

(b) An attorney shall not enter into a contingent fee arrangement without first having advised the client of the right and afforded the client an opportunity to retain the attorney under an arrangement for compensation on the basis of the reasonable value of the services.

(c) In any matter where a client's claim for damages is based upon the alleged tortious conduct of another, including products liability claims and claims among family members that are subject to Part V of these Rules but excluding statutorily based discrimination and employment claims, and the client is not a subrogee, an attorney shall not contract for, charge, or collect a contingent fee in excess of the following limits:

(1) 33 1/3% on the first $500,000 recovered;
(2) 30% on the next $500,000 recovered;
(3) 25% on the next $500,000 recovered;
(4) 20% on the next $500,000 recovered; and
(5) on all amounts recovered in excess of the above by application for reasonable fee in accordance with the provisions of paragraph (f) hereof; and
(6) where the amount recovered is for the benefit of a client who was a minor or mentally incapacitated when the contingent fee arrangement was made, the foregoing limits shall apply, except that the fee on any amount recovered by settlement without trial shall not exceed 25%.

(d) The permissible fee provided for in paragraph (c) shall be computed on the net sum recovered after deducting disbursements in connection with the institution and prosecution of the claim, whether advanced by the attorney or by the client, including investigation expenses, expenses for expert or other testimony or evidence, the cost of briefs and transcripts on appeal, and any interest included in a judgment pursuant to R. 4:42-11(b); but no deduction need be made for post-judgment interest or for liens, assignments or claims in favor of hospitals or for medical care and treatment by doctors and nurses, or similar items. The permissible fee shall include legal services rendered on any appeal or review proceeding or on any retrial, but this shall not be deemed to require an attorney to take an appeal. When joint representation is undertaken in both the direct and derivative action, or when a claim for wrongful death is joined with a claim on behalf of a decedent, the contingent fee shall be calculated on the aggregate sum of the recovery.

(e) Paragraph (c) of this rule is intended to fix maximum permissible fees and does not preclude an attorney from entering into a contingent fee arrangement providing for, or from charging or collecting a contingent fee below such limits. In all cases contingent fees charged or collected must conform to RPC 1.5(a).

(f) If at the conclusion of a matter an attorney considers the fee permitted by paragraph (c) to be inadequate, an application on written notice to the client may be made to the Assignment Judge for the hearing and determining of a reasonable fee in light of all the circumstances. This rule shall not preclude the exercise of a client's existing right to a court review of the reasonableness of an attorney's fee.

(g) Where the amount of the contingent fee is limited by the provisions of paragraph (c) of this rule, the contingent fee arrangement shall be in writing, signed both by the attorney and the client, and a signed duplicate shall be given to the client. Upon conclusion of the matter resulting in a recovery, the attorney shall prepare and furnish the client with a signed closing statement.

(h) Calculation of Fee in Structured Settlements. As used herein the term "structured settlement" refers to the payment of any settlement between the parties or judgment entered pursuant to a proceeding approved by the Court, the terms of which provide for the payment of the funds to be received by the plaintiff on an installment basis. For purposes of paragraph (c), the basis for calculation of a contingent fee shall be the value of the structured settlement as herein defined. Value shall consist of any cash payment made upon consummation of the settlement plus the actual cost to the party making the settlement of the deferred payment aspects thereof. In the event that the party paying the settlement does not purchase the deferred payment component, the actual cost thereof shall be the actual cost assigned by that party to that component. For further purposes of this rule, the party making the settlement offer shall, at the time the offer is made, disclose to the party receiving the settlement offer its actual cost and, if it does not purchase the deferred payment aspect of the settlement, the factors and assumptions used by it in assigning actual cost.

(i) Calculation of Fee in Settlement of Class or Multiple Party Actions. When representation is undertaken on behalf of several persons whose respective claims, whether or not joined in one action, arise out of the same transaction or set of facts or involve substantially identical liability issues, the contingent fee shall be calculated on the basis of the aggregate sum of all recoveries, whether by judgment, settlement or both, and shall be charged to the clients in proportion to the recovery of each. Counsel may, however, make application for modification of the fee pursuant to paragraph (f) of this rule in appropriate cases.

RPC I:8(e) OF THE RULES OF PROFESSIONAL CONDUCT

(e) A lawyer shall not provide financial assistance to a client in connection with pending or contemplated litigation, except that:

(1) a lawyer may advance court costs and expenses of litigation, the repayment of which may be contingent on the outcome of the matter; and

(2) a lawyer representing an indigent client may pay court costs and expenses of litigation on behalf of the client; and

(3) A non-profit organization authorized under R. I:2I-I(e) may provide financial assistance to indigent clients whom it is representing without fee.

39:6A-8 TORT EXEMPTION: THE LIMITATION ON LAWSUIT THRESHOLD

8. Tort exemption; limitation on the right to noneconomic loss. One of the following two tort options shall be elected, in accordance with section 14.1 of P.L.1983, c.362 (C.39:6A-8.1), by any named insured required to maintain personal injury protection coverage pursuant to section 4 of P.L.1972, c.70 (C.39:6A-4):

a. **Limitation on lawsuit option.** Every owner, registrant, operator or occupant of an automobile to which section 4 of P.L.1972, c.70 (C.39:6A-4), personal injury protection coverage, section 4 of P.L.1998, c.21 (C.39:6A-3.1), medical expense benefits coverage, or section 45 of P.L.2003, c.89 (C.39:6A-3.3) regardless of fault, applies, and every person or organization legally responsible for his acts or omissions, is hereby exempted from tort liability for noneconomic loss to a person who is subject to this subsection and who is either a person who is required to maintain personal injury protection coverage pursuant to section 4 of P.L.1972, c.70 (C.39:6A-4), medical expense benefits pursuant to section 4 of P.L.1998, c.21 (C.39:6A-3.1) or benefits pursuant to section 45 of P.L.2003, c.89 (C.39:6A-3.3), or is a person who has a right to receive benefits under section 4 of P.L.1972, c.70 (C.39:6A-4), section 4 of P.L.1998, c.21 (C.39:6A-3.1) or section 45 of P.L.2003, c.89 (C.39:6A-3.3), as a result of bodily injury, arising out of the ownership, operation, maintenance or use of such automobile in this State, <u>unless that person has sustained a bodily injury which results in death; dismem-</u>

berment; significant disfigurement or significant scarring; displaced fractures; loss of a fetus; or a permanent injury within a reasonable degree of medical probability, other than scarring or disfigurement. An injury shall be considered permanent when the body part or organ, or both, has not healed to function normally and will not heal to function normally with further medical treatment. For the purposes of this subsection, "physician" means a physician as defined in section 5 of P.L.1939, c.115 (C.45:9-5.1).

In order to satisfy the tort option provisions of this subsection, the plaintiff shall, within 60 days following the date of the answer to the complaint by the defendant, provide the defendant with a certification from the licensed treating physician or a board-certified licensed physician to whom the plaintiff was referred by the treating physician. The certification shall state, under penalty of perjury, that the plaintiff has sustained an injury described above. The certification shall be based on and refer to objective clinical evidence, which may include medical testing, except that any such testing shall be performed in accordance with medical protocols pursuant to subsection a. of section 4 of P.L.1972, c.70 (C.39:6A-4) and the use of valid diagnostic tests administered in accordance with section 12 of P.L.1998, c.21 (C.39:6A-4.7). Such testing may not be experimental in nature or dependent entirely upon subjective patient response. The court may grant no more than one additional period not to exceed 60 days to file the certification pursuant to this subsection upon a finding of good cause.

A person is guilty of a crime of the fourth degree if that person purposefully or knowingly makes, or causes to be made, a false, fictitious, fraudulent, or misleading statement of material fact in, or omits a material fact from, or causes a material fact to be omitted from, any certification filed pursuant to this subsection. Notwithstanding the provisions of subsection e. of N.J.S.2C:44-1, the court shall deal with a person who has been convicted of a violation of this subsection by imposing a sentence of imprisonment unless, having regard to the character and condition of the person, the court is of the opinion that imprisonment would be a serious injustice which overrides the need to deter such conduct by others. If the court imposes a noncustodial or probationary sentence, such sentence shall not become final for 10 days in order to permit the appeal of such sentence by the prosecution. Nothing in this subsection a. shall preclude an indictment and conviction for any other offense defined by the laws of this State. In addition, any professional license held by the person shall be forfeited according to the procedures established by section 4 of P.L.1997, c.353 (C.2C:51-5); or

b. No limitation on lawsuit option. As an alternative to the basic tort option specified in subsection a. of this section, every owner, registrant, operator, or occupant of an automobile to which section 4 of P.L.1972, c.70 (C.39:6A-4), personal injury protection coverage, section 4 of P.L.1998, c.21 (C.39:6A-3.1), medical expense benefits coverage, or section 45 of P.L.2003, c.89 (C.39:6A-3.3), regardless of fault, applies, and every person or organization legally responsible for his acts or omissions, shall be liable for noneconomic loss to a person who is subject to this subsection and who is either a person who is required to maintain the coverage mandated by P.L.1972, c.70 (C.39:6A-1 et seq.) or is a person who has a right to receive benefits under section 4 of that act (C.39:6A-4), as a result of bodily injury, arising out of the ownership, operation, maintenance or use of such automobile in this State.

The tort option provisions of subsection b. of this section shall also apply to the right to recover for noneconomic loss of any person eligible for benefits pursuant to section 4 of P.L.1972, c.70 (C.39:6A-4), section 4 of P.L.1998, c.21 (C.39:6A-3.1) or section 45 of P.L.2003, c.89 (C.39:6A-3.3) but who is not required to maintain personal injury protection coverage pursuant to section 4 of P.L.1972, c.70 (C.39:6A-4), medical expense benefits coverage pursuant to section 4 of P.L.1998, c.21 (C.39:6A-3.1) or benefits pursuant to section 45 of P.L.2003, c.89 (C.39:6A-3.3) and is not an immediate family member, as defined in section 14.1 of P.L.1983, c.362 (C.39:6A-8.1), under a standard automobile insurance policy or basic automobile insurance policy.

The tort option provisions of subsection a. of this section shall also apply to any person subject to section 14 of P.L.1985, c.520 (C.39:6A-4.5) and to every named insured and any other person to whom the benefits of the special automobile insurance policy provided in section 45 of P.L.2003, c.89 (C.39:6A-3.3) or the medical expense benefits of the basic automobile insurance policy pursuant to section 4 of P.L.1998, c.21 (C.39:6A-3.1) apply whether or not the person has elected the optional $10,000 liability coverage insuring against loss resulting from liability imposed by law for bodily injury or death provided for in subsection c. of section 4 of P.L.1998, c.21 (C.39:6A-3.1).

The tort option provisions of subsections a. and b. of this section as provided in this 1998 amendatory and supplementary act shall apply to automobile insurance policies issued or renewed on or after the effective date of P.L.1998, c.21 (C.39:6A-1.1 et al.) and as otherwise provided by law. L.1972,c.70,s.8; amended 1972, c.203, s.6; 1983, c.362, s.14; 1985, c.520, s.15; 1988, c.119, s.6; 1990, c.8, s.9; 1998, c.21, s.11; 2003, c.89, s.52

JURY INSTRUCTIONS REGARDING WRONGFUL DEATH DAMAGES

8.43 WRONGFUL DEATH (3/10)

The plaintiff brings this lawsuit as the representative of the survivors of the decedent, [*insert decedent's name*]. On behalf of the survivors, the plaintiff asserts that the defendant was responsible for the decedent's death and seeks money damages from the defendant for the actual financial losses the survivors have suffered, and will suffer in the future, as a result of the decedent's death.

What Is Not Recoverable

A. In this category of damages, you are not to consider any physical injuries or suffering that the decedent may have sustained, such as pain and suffering or disability

B. You are also not to consider any emotional distress, anguish or grief the survivors may have suffered as a result of the decedent's death, or any loss of emotional satisfaction the survivors may have derived from the society and companionship of the decedent. These matters, although very real and distressing, cannot be considered in determining the extent of the financial loss suffered by the survivors.

What Is Recoverable

Financial loss includes not only the actual monies the decedent would have earned and contributed for the benefit of the survivors, but also the reasonable value of the services, assistance, care, training, guidance, advice, counsel and companionship the survivors would have received from the decedent had he/she lived.

A. With regard to the decedent's earnings, you should consider the net earnings after taxes as of the time of the decedent's death. You should also give due regard to any evidence concerning the decedent's potential future income during the balance of his/her working life expectancy. The income figure you use should be net income, that is, income after taxes. This is because net income represents that portion of the decedent's income which would have been available for the benefit of the decedent's survivors. Net income also includes fringe benefits, such as monies the decedent would have obtained in the form of employer contribution to a retirement plan. Since money used for the decedent's personal maintenance and expenses would not have been available for the benefit of the survivors, you must subtract the decedent's personal expenses from the net income. You must find to what extent the decedent's net earnings were necessary for his/her personal needs and deduct that amount from the net income.

B. You may also consider the benefit the survivors would have received from the decedent in the form of services, assistance, guidance and training. In making such an award, you must determine the reasonable value of the services or benefits that will be lost by reason of the decedent's death.

C. In addition to the loss of anticipated direct financial contributions from the decedent to the survivors, as I explained previously, you should also consider the pecuniary value of the loss of the decedent's anticipated services to the survivors. This may include things such as chores the decedent would have performed including household chores, babysitting, etc. You should also consider the value of the loss of the companionship, advice and guidance of the deceased as the survivors grow older. You must remember, however, that your award for damages for these losses will be confined to their financial value and should not include any amount of emotional loss.

Bear in mind that in fixing an award for services, companionship, care, advice and counsel, you must distinguish between their emotional value and their financial or economic value. We recognize that [children, parents, spouse] may provide valuable services such as companionship, care, advice and guidance over time as the survivor(s) face(s) advanced age or declining health. Remember, however, that no pecuniary value may be attached to the emotional satisfaction gained by the parent, spouse or child if the deceased has performed these services.

Perhaps the best way to describe the type of services that can be compensable under the category of loss of care are those substantially similar to the services provided by paid "companions" or "homemakers" who are often hired by the aged or the infirm, or substantially equivalent to services provided by nurses or practical nurses. Companionship in this sense, however, will not include true nursing services unless you find that the decedent had or was likely to have special training. The value of these services must be confined to what the marketplace would pay a stranger with similar qualifications to the deceased to perform such services. In interpreting the criteria of "similar qualifications," you may also attach a financial value to the knowledge of the survivors' likes, dislikes, abilities and habits which the decedent may have possessed.

Under the category of loss of the decedent's guidance, advice and counsel to the survivors, we are speaking only of its financial element. It is the loss of guidance, advice and counsel we all need from time to time in particular situations, for specific purposes, such as in making a business decision, or a decision affecting one's life generally, or even advice and counsel needed to relieve depression or personal dilemmas. It must be the kind of advice and guidance that could be purchased from a business advisor, a therapist, or a trained counselor, for instance. It is not the loss simply of the exchange of views, no matter how perceptive, when the survivor and loved ones are together nor is it the loss of the pleasure which accompanies such an exchange between family members because, again, emotional loss is not involved in this computation.

You must decide what services the decedent would have rendered to the survivors, as well as the value of these services. The survivors do not have to prove that they would have in fact purchased such companionship and advice after the decedent's death; it is sufficient that the decedent would have rendered it to them if he/she had lived. To the extent that it is relevant to the issue of the services the decedent would have provided, you should also consider the decedent's character, personality, habits and customs as well as his/her relationship with the survivors.

As part of your deliberations in this regard, you should also consider the age and general health of the decedent and the survivors, since this may affect the period of time over which it would be reasonably expected that the decedent would have rendered the services to the survivors. You can consider the life expectancy and the work-life expectancy of the decedent at the time of death and the life expectancy of the survivor or survivors.

Compensation

If you find that plaintiff is entitled to an award, the amount recoverable is comprised of two parts:
a. the amount of the financial loss to date; and
b. the present value of any future financial loss.

I. Past Loss

Once you have decided that the plaintiff is entitled to recover, the first thing you must determine is the amount of the financial loss from the date of death to the present. Financial loss means both categories of financial loss which I just described and the reasonable value of the benefits or services the decedent would have given the survivors.

2. Future Losses
A. Preliminary Charge to be Given Before Any Expert Testimony

In this phase of the case, you are about to hear expert opinion testimony on certain economic claims made. You will be the final judges of the reliability of these experts' projections of future economic losses. Any bottom line figure offered by the expert will be based on certain assumptions that the expert will make concerning probable future economic trends.

In evaluating the reliability of the expert's projections, you may consider the cross-examination by the attorneys and also any evidence presented by the opposing parties on this issue such as other expert testimony. At this state of the case, you should keep an open mind regarding the reliability of these bottom-line figures and not given them automatic acceptance. I repeat, it will be your responsibility and your responsibility alone to determine at the close of the case the amount of economic losses suffered by the plaintiff, based upon all the credible evidence you choose to accept on this question.

B. Final Charge to be Given at Conclusion of Case if There is No Expert Testimony

Plaintiff also seeks to recover for financial support and services that will be lost in the future. Obviously, the time period covering the survivor's future losses cannot go beyond that point when it was expected that the deceased and/or the survivor would live. The ability of an adult to render services may decrease with age or increase with age in the case of a child. You can take into account both life expectancy and work-life expectancy.

But you should be aware that the figures that you have been given on life expectancy and work-life expectancy are only statistical averages. Do not treat them as necessary or fixed rules, since they are general estimates. Use them with caution and use you sound judgment in taking them into account.

For future loss of financial support, as well as past loss of financial support, you must base your decision on probable net earnings, the take-home pay, the amount left after taxes are deducted. It is the burden of the plaintiff to prove, by a preponderance of the evidence, the deceased's net income and the probable loss of future support and services.

In deciding what plaintiff's future losses are, understand that the law does not require of you mathematical exactness. Rather, you must use sound judgment based on reasonable probability.

C. Effects of Interest and Inflation on Future Earnings

Once you have decided how much money plaintiff will lose in the future, you must then consider the effects of inflation and interest. As to inflation, you should consider the effects it probably will have in reducing the purchasing power of money. Any award for future losses may be increased to account for losses in the purchasing power of that money because of inflation. The consideration of interest requires that you should not just award plaintiff the exact amount of money that he/she will be losing in the future. The survivors will have that money now even though he/she/they will not have incurred the loss of that money until some time in the future. And that means that survivors will be able to invest the money and earn interest on it now even though he/she/they otherwise would not have had that money to invest until some future date.

To make up for this, you must make an adjustment for the survivors having the money available now even though the loss will not be experienced until the future. This adjustment is known as discounting, and discounting gives you the value of the money that you get now instead of getting it at some future time. In other words, it gives you the present value or present worth in a single lump sum of money which otherwise was going to be received over a number of years at so much per year.

Your goal is to create a fund of money, which, if paid today, will fairly compensate plaintiff for his or her future loss of earnings. In arriving at the amount of that fund – the present value of future losses – you should consider the interest the fund will probably earn in future years; the probable amount by which taxation on the interest might decrease the money available to plaintiff and the effect of inflation in decreasing the purchase power of money. The higher the interest rate you believe the fund will earn in future years, the lower will be the amount of the fund needed to fairly compensate plaintiff for future earnings. On the other hand, the higher the probable rate of inflation in future years, the higher twill be the amount of the fund needed to fairly compensate plaintiff. It is possible that the interest earned in the future could be offset exactly by the rate of inflation in which event these factors could cancel each other out and you could award the net lost wages for the appropriate number of years without any adjustment.

D. Final Charge to be Given at Conclusion of Case if There was Expert Testimony on the "Bottom Line" You have heard an expert (or an expert for each side) discuss the present value of plaintiff's future losses including projections as to future interest, including its tax consequences, and inflation rates. You may consider some, all, or none of the opinions of the experts in determining a fair figure to compensate plaintiff for future losses. The experts have also given you their "bottom line" figures as to decedent's future lost earnings. As I told you previously, you need not give any of these "bottom line" figures automatic acceptance. You are free to determine, based on all the evidence, including the expert testimony you choose to accept, what amount of dollars will fairly compensate plaintiff for his/her future losses.

3. Medical and Funeral Expenses

The plaintiff is also entitled to an award for reasonable and related medical expenses and funeral expenses